...BUT GOD

Trials, Testimonies, and Triumph

By

Suzanne C. Buck

...BUT GOD: Testimonies, Trials, and Triumph
by: Suzanne C. Buck, Copyright © 2024

ISBN: 978-1-947288-78-2

All rights reserved solely by the author. The author certifies that except where designated, all contents are original and do not infringe upon the legal rights of any other person or work. No part of this book may be reproduced in any form without the permission of the author and the publisher.

Scripture quotations marked **NASB** are taken from the Holy Bible, New American Standard Bible®, Copyright © 1960, 1962, 1963, 1968, 1971,1972, 1973, 1975, 1977, 1995 by The Lockman Foundation Used by permission." (www.Lockman.org). Scripture quotations marked **NIV** are taken from the New International Version®, NIV®. Copyright © 1973, 1978, 1984, 2011 by Biblica, Inc.™ Used by permission of Zondervan. All rights reserved worldwide. www.zondervan.com. Scripture quotations marked **KJV** are taken from the King James Version of the Bible. Scripture quotations marked **NKJV**™ are taken from the New King James Version®. Copyright © 1982 by Thomas Nelson, Inc. Used by permission. All rights reserved. Scripture quotations are from the **ESV**® Bible (The Holy Bible, English Standard Version®), © 2001 by Crossway, a publishing ministry of Good News Publishers. Used by permission. All rights reserved. Scripture quotations marked (**NLT**) are taken from the Holy Bible, New Living Translation, copyright ©1996, 2004, 2015 by Tyndale House Foundation. Used by permission of Tyndale House Publishers, Carol Stream, Illinois 60188. All rights reserved. Scripture quotations marked (**TLB**) are taken from The Living Bible, copyright © 1971 by Tyndale House Foundation. Used by permission of Tyndale House Publishers, Carol Stream, Illinois 60188. All rights reserved.

Printed in the United States

10 9 8 7 6 5 4 3 2 1

Cover design by: Legacy Design Inc: Legacydesigninc@gmail.com

Published by Life To Legacy, LLC
P.O. 1239
Matteson, IL 60443
708-272-4444
www.Life2Legacy.com
Life2legacybooks@att.net

TABLE OF CONTENTS

Dedication	5
1. Suzie's Miraculous Healing and Deliverance	9
2. Heather Honey	17
3. Hannah's Prayer	25
4. Whitney's Bicycle Accident	33
5. God's Grace for Wayne	37
6. Keithe's Bump in the Road	41
7. Andrea's and Heather's Car Accident	45
8. God's Mercy and Grace for Andrea	57
9. Wayne's Heart	65
10. Wayne's Faith Challenge	71
11. Andrea's Prodigal Journey	83
12. The End of Her Journey	97
13. Me and My Shadow	107
14. Where Did He Come From?	145
My Testimony	151
Suzie's Favorite Scriptures	152
About the Author	157

DEDICATION

This book was written to encourage all who have been or are going through the most difficult experiences a person can go through, and those who have experienced some of the most amazing answers to their prayers. To those going through the dark valleys, I hope you will find encouragement to hold on to God, and His Word until the light, and the answers come. I can assure you they will come, because God is faithful and trustworthy. You are not alone. You are loved.

I dedicate this book first to God my Father, to Jesus Christ my Lord and Savior, and to the Holy Spirit my teacher, counselor, and comforter for giving me the title for this book over three years ago. The Lord continued to prod me to sit at my computer and write. He would nudge me more when my pastor, Dr. Chauncey Fourte, would be preaching, and it seemed that every other sentence he said began or finished with 'BUT GOD…' I am deeply grateful.

I also dedicate this book to my husband, Wayne Buck, who continues to support me in whatever I sense the Lord is leading me to be involved in. You are my hero, and the love of my life. Thank you for your encouragement and assistance as I was writing this book.

I dedicate this book to my 5 children, Heather Buck, Jennifer Jones, Whitney Coleman, Andrea Milligan, and Jonathan Buck. I also include my nephew, Stephen Allain. Each of them has allowed me to share some of the most difficult events of their lives, and their celebrations. Sometimes it's been their strength, and courage that has deeply touched my heart, and shown me how to go on.

I want to thank my friend Beth Montgomery for driving down to Muskogee and retrieving my manuscript on the computer when I thought I had lost it. My knowledge of the computer has been minimal, but Beth saved my day.

Lastly, but certainly not least, I dedicate this book to Elder Jocelyn Scales, Apostle Peggy Seals, Prophetess Gwendolyn Fourte, Dr. Chauncey Fourte, Jessika Tate, Imani Thomas from Kingdom Church in Broken Arrow, Oklahoma, and

my faithful friend Phyllis Griffin, for the years of friendship, teachings, encouragement, direction, prayers, and love. I'm deeply grateful for learning how to praise and worship God in the dark places. If it wasn't for these influencers in my life I wouldn't know the depth of my Savior's love.
—Suzanne C. Buck "Suzie"

Suzanne C. Buck

Love is patient, love is kind. It does not envy, it does not boast, It is not proud. It is not rude, It is not self-seeking, It is not easily angered, It keeps no record of wrongs. Love does not delight in evil But rejoices with the truth. It always protects, always trusts, Always hopes, always perseveres. Love Never Fails.
1 Corinthians 13:4-8

1
Suzie's Miraculous Healing, and Deliverance

Mother's Day 1974 was a very emotional day for me. I was very depressed because a dear friend suddenly died and left four little daughters without their mom. However, the emotional pain wasn't my only challenge. I had a severe stomach ulcer and had just gotten out of the hospital. My doctor told me that I needed to reduce the stress in my life, and that would take care of the ulcer. He said I needed to prioritize putting God first, my family second, and my college classes third. I had one daughter, Heather, and I was finishing my bachelor's degree in Speech-Language Pathology. Admittedly, I was frustrated by the doctor's remarks. BUT GOD had a different plan for my life.

My twin sister, Kitty, had been calling me and telling me I had to get saved, and give my life to Jesus. We were Episcopalians, and there wasn't any emphasis placed on getting saved. My sister's persistence reminded me of my boyfriend, Tom Lutz, from high school. I went with him to his father's Baptist Church several times, and his father had spoken to me about getting 'saved' and giving my life to Jesus. I really didn't understand what that meant. I had always loved Jesus. I was confirmed in the Episcopal Church as a child. So, when Kitty started hounding me about salvation, it annoyed me. When I talked with my mom about the ulcer, ironically, she said I needed to pray and give it up to the Lord. Going to the Lord was coming from every side. Maybe God was trying to tell me something.

So, one night I took a shower and just started crying and calling out to God to heal me and truly cleanse me right there in the shower. I felt relieved, like a burden had been lifted off my shoulders.

On another occasion Kitty called, just after my friend had died and I poured out my heart to her. She said I needed to watch The 700 Club on television. That was the evening of Mother's Day.

My husband, Wayne, was asleep on the couch, and I turned on **The 700 Club**. Pat Robertson was the host. They talked to different people about Jesus and how He was working in their lives. Then he asked the television audience to pray with him. I was very intent on listening to his prayer. After the prayer he said, "Someone has a severe stomach ulcer, and as I say these things you're going to feel them. God is touching your stomach and healing it. The power of God is surging from the top of your head to the tip of your toes, and you will have no more pain. You are healed!" Oh my God! I literally felt this huge hand touch my stomach! It was like heat and electricity surging throughout my body. I was shaking all over and crying from this amazing, miraculous encounter with God!

Wayne woke up and asked, "What is going on?" I told him God had touched and healed me. He got up from the couch and said, "If you're healed go eat an onion." I responded, "You don't put God to the test!" I had no knowledge of the Bible, yet what I quoted was actually a verse found in Luke 4:12, "And Jesus answered and said to him, "It is said, 'you shall not put the Lord your God to the test.'" Wayne couldn't quite comprehend what I was going through, so he retreated and went up the stairs to bed. I continued to weep and praise and thank God for this miraculous healing! I later went to bed but could not sleep. The presence and glory of God was so strong and hovered over me all night! I continued to weep and worship the Almighty God. I felt the intensity of God's love for me all night long.

The next morning, I got up and fed and dressed Heather and took her to the babysitter. I drove to meet my supervisor of Speech-Language Therapy. As we drove to a school for observation, I could not help but tell her what had happened to me. She just said, "That's nice." She did not understand one bit of what I described to her. I felt God's presence all day as we worked. I just wanted to get home and tell Wayne again, and call Kitty.

I knew I was healed! Prior to my healing I had only been drinking cream for my stomach, but this night I made meat loaf with onions. When Wayne arrived home, he asked what I had fixed for dinner. I told him I fixed meat loaf. He replied, "You can't eat that because of your stomach!" I said, "Don't you remember what I told you last night?" He said, "NO!" I told him again that God had touched my stomach and healed me! When we sat down to eat, he watched me eat with no pain. Wayne didn't know what to say. I never had another stomach pain or ulcer after that.

I made an appointment with my doctor. When I told him what had happened, he shouted 'HALLELUJAH!' He did another test and verified that I had indeed received a miraculous healing! It was just like what is said in the Scriptures, "And God confirmed the message by giving signs, wonders, and various miracles, and gifts of the Holy Spirit whenever he chose" (Hebrews 2:4, NLT).

The following weeks I just felt wrapped up in the Spirit. Everything felt brighter in every way. The colors were vibrant, and nature became such a wondrous miracle. All I wanted to do was to read my Bible. I started out reading the Gospel of Matthew and kept reading through the entire New Testament.

A couple of weeks later I was seeking God to set me free from a terrible nicotine addiction. I smoked at least three packs of cigarettes a day. I hated smoking but I was unable to quit. The addiction was so real. Every time I tried to quit smoking I would get sick at my stomach, have cramps in my stomach, and would go back to smoking. I pleaded with God to deliver me.

I was then told about The Full Gospel Businessmen's Fellowship meeting and worship. I was told they always had a motivational speaker and wonderful worship. I asked Wayne to come with me, and he reluctantly said okay. There were about sixty men and women at the meeting and the worship and message moved me. On the last song I raised my hands to the Lord, and had my eyes closed. Suddenly I had a ticker tape going across my mind; it said, "DELIVERED FROM CIGARETTES!" I was stunned! Then I heard a voice say, "You're gonna want a cigarette as soon as you get in the car!" It was the devil's voice. BUT GOD had another plan for me, and I had to decide which message I was going to agree with. Immediately I said, "NO" to the voice, and I began praising and thanking God for His deliverance from the craving, and addiction to cigarettes! It was instantaneous! I was so thrilled and grateful! "Agree with God, and be at peace; thereby good will come to you" (Job 22:2, ESV).

Two weeks later Wayne and I were sitting on the couch watching TV when he said, "Pass me the ashtray please." I said, "Wayne, God delivered me from cigarettes at that meeting we went to. I haven't smoked since then." He just stared at me. He knew how addicted I was, BUT GOD did another miracle for me! I haven't smoked since.

With all that was happening in our family my youngest sister, Candy, decided to go to Atlanta to visit Kitty, to see what she "had gotten in to." She got saved and filled with the Spirit! Then my mom and dad went to Atlanta, and they got saved, water baptized and filled with the Spirit!

I was filled with the Holy Spirit as I was fixing dinner one night. I just started saying 'I love you Jesus' over and over, and suddenly these weird sounds started coming out of my mouth. "...And everyone present was filled with the Holy Spirit and began speaking in other languages, as the Holy Spirit gave them this ability" (Acts 2:4, TLB). It was amazing knowing that the Holy Spirit had come upon me like this. I was speaking in tongues and able to pray in this holy language any time I wanted to.

Shortly after this we drove to Oklahoma to visit our family. Candy and I decided to get baptized in the river by the pastor of Abundant Life Church.

What a glorious feeling of dying to the old, and raising up in the new. "And Peter said to them, 'Repent and be baptized every one of you in the name of Jesus Christ for the forgiveness of your sins, and you will receive the gift of the Holy Spirit'" (Acts 2:38, ESV).

At one point after we had moved back to Oklahoma from Pennsylvania my oldest sister Keithe came to visit since she had heard about the different family members getting saved and filled with the Holy Spirit. She came to the church that all of my family attended. She wept through the whole service. Afterward the pastor prayed with her, and she gave her heart to Jesus Christ. She was also baptized in the river, and in the Holy Spirit.

A couple years later Wayne, my husband, and Rick, Candy's husband, both experienced salvation, water baptism, and the infilling or baptism of the Holy Spirit.

My healing and my family all being saved, baptized, and filled with the Holy Spirit was a domino effect that is indescribable, except to say it was outrageously glorious!

2
Heather Honey

Heather was our first child. When she was born, I knew something was not quite right. She weighed 7 pounds and 2 ounces and was born on 6/4/1972. Her feet and hands were very puffy, yet she was a small baby. From the beginning she had eating problems with nursing and with formula. She had a lot of projectile vomiting. It was very scary to be holding her, and trying to burp her when she would do this projectile vomiting that would explode out of this tiny baby's mouth and shoot across the room almost emptying her stomach. I talked to my sister Keithe, who was studying to be a nurse, and asked her for advice. She had two little girls, and I thought she would know what to do.

Everything she suggested and what the doctor recommended did not help. Keithe asked me to bring Heather to her home in Virginia, outside of Washington, D.C. Heather continued to have the projectile vomiting at Keithe's home. So Keithe decided we needed to take Heather to the Children's Clinic in Washington, D.C.

When we arrived at the clinic the room was filled with parents and children waiting to see doctors. We sat there for over six hours before a young doctor from Oklahoma (my home state), Dr. Marilyn McCaffry, called us in. She asked detailed questions about Heather and our concerns. Then she did a 'buckle smear' from the inside of my cheek, and one from inside Heather's cheek. She said she was sending these off to a special lab in California, and she would have results in about six weeks. She then told us that she suspected that Heather was born with Turner's Syndrome. She had recently been studying about this, and said Heather had several of the symptoms.

She explained to us that Turner's Syndrome is the absence of one X chromosome in each of her blood cells. Females typically have 2 X chromosomes, and boys have an X and a Y chromosome.

She suspected Heather had one X. She didn't think it was hereditary but just one of those happenings. This was very shocking for us! The doctor also gave us some instructions that helped with the projectile vomiting.

So, Heather and I flew home, and Wayne and I talked about this possibility. We were both very sad, and felt that somehow, we were responsible for this. The results were sent to us, and they verified Heather had Turner's Syndrome, but it was atypical. This meant she did not have all the standard symptoms of Turner's Syndrome, which were a webbed neck, and heart problems. She did have ear problems, and later in life she had to have a tympanoplasty to replace an ear drum. Heather did have a short stature, and she would not be able to have children. Turner's Syndrome kids grow up to have a great love for children, which proved true for Heather. We thought of the future and how we would help Heather understand her diagnosis as she grew up without letting it impact her self-esteem.

When Heather was eight years old the National Institutes of Health contacted us to see if Heather could participate in their research of Turner's Syndrome. We agreed, and at that point we were flown to the National Institutes of Health monthly for the next three years. Heather was in a study group with either hormones or placebo. We never knew which group she was assigned.

It was a blessing in several ways to be flown free of charge to Virginia because we were able to visit with my oldest sister Keithe, and her family almost monthly. Heather became close to her cousins, her aunt, and uncle. Occasionally my mom would take Heather so she could visit my sister and her family. Sometimes Wayne would take Heather, and they would fly in the morning and fly back to Oklahoma in the late afternoon.

Heather was a very happy child, and very helpful with her sisters. She loved to sing and had a good singing voice. When she was 12 years old, she was only 4 foot 7 inches tall. She decided to sing a solo at church one Sunday. Its words said, "I'm only 4 foot 7 and I'm going to Heaven, and it makes me feel 10 feet tall!" Heather oozed with joy as a child and made many friends. "The joy of the Lord is your strength" (Nehemiah 8:10, NLT). It's very interesting that Heather's name means "joyful spirit," and she embodied that.

When Heather was twelve and a half the National Institutes of Health (NIH) without warning, concluded the study. We were shocked and felt cut off. We were wondering what we should do now? BUT GOD had a good plan for Heather.

> "For I know the plans I have for you, declares the Lord, plans to prosper you and not to harm you, plans to give you hope and a future."
> Jeremiah 29:11, NIV

We asked the Institute what we could do for Heather. They at least hooked us up with Dr. Don Wilson at the Children's Hospital in Tulsa, Oklahoma. He was a Geneticist and an Endocrinologist. He oversaw Heather for several years. One day we got a call from Dr. Wilson that he had contacted a pharmaceutical company who was willing to send us, free of charge, growth hormone injections that we would administer to Heather. The medicine was worth about $10,000 each month which she took for about three years.

What a miracle! Who does such a thing for a young girl? Only by the favor and loving heart of God could this have happened! "And we know that all things work together for good to those who love God, to those who are the called according to His purpose" (Romans 8:28, NKJV). During those three years she grew to be 5 foot 2 inches tall. She also grew breasts which, according to the research, wasn't supposed to happen. The plan of God was truly unfolding in Heather's life. It was a thrill to see God working.

Heather was such a special child. When she was three years old Wayne and I were talking about returning to Muskogee, Oklahoma where his mom and my parents lived. Wayne had not yet given his heart to Jesus, but I was praying for the will of God to direct us if we were supposed to move.

I always had Heather agreeing with me in prayer. Once Wayne and I decided it would be best to move back to Oklahoma, he flew down for an interview with a district director of an insurance company. Heather, baby sister Jennifer, and I were at home in Pennsylvania. I was ironing, and Jennifer was asleep. Heather kept asking me when will Daddy be home. I finally instructed her to go into her bedroom and pray to God about Daddy coming home. About five minutes later, Heather came out of her room, and said, "I prayed to God about Daddy coming home." I said, "Okay, so what did God say?" She immediately started speaking in tongues, and then said, "That's what He said." I was shocked! Heather frequently went with me to my Bible study group which prayed in the Spirit during our meetings. I don't remember her ever speaking in tongues again until she was older.

> *"All of them were filled with the Holy Spirit and began to speak in other tongues as the Spirit enabled them" Acts 2:4, NIV*

After we had moved to Muskogee and Wayne had taken the insurance agent job, my parents felt lead of the Lord to move outside of town on an 80-acre ranch with lots of hills and trees around it. Daddy dedicated this ranch to the Lord, and he knew he'd need God to take care of it. He and my mom moved from the Country Club area to this ranch that he named "Hallelujah Hill." Wayne, the kids, and I went to the ranch every weekend to help Dad and Mom for four years.

One time after a very hard day of working and building fences, we were driving home, and Wayne stopped at a traffic light. Heather and I had been singing Jesus' songs, and suddenly she popped up between Wayne and me and said, "Daddy, do you have Jesus in your heart?" Wayne didn't answer. Again, Heather looked at Wayne and said "Daddy, do you have Jesus in your heart?" This time Wayne made a quick grunt. Heather looked at me and said, "Mama, is that a yes or a, no?" I told her I didn't know, BUT GOD had used this little child to prick the heart of her daddy. Within that very year Wayne gave his heart to Jesus. What an awesome God! "…and a little child shall lead them" (Isaiah 11:6, NIV).

3
Hannah's Prayer

In 1982, Wayne and I had our fourth daughter, Andrea. She was such a joy as each of our other three daughters had also been. Each of our girls looked different, and each was beautiful. Each of our girls had different personalities, too. When they were young, Heather and Andrea both had blonde hair, Jennifer had light auburn hair, and Whitney had dark brown hair. We desperately loved our girls, but I had always wanted a son.

I wanted a son because I had wanted a brother when I was young, but my parents had four daughters. After Wayne and I were married I really thought about having a son. Wayne had a son from his first marriage, but for various reasons, he hadn't been allowed to be involved much in his son's life. I wanted a son for Wayne's sake, even though Wayne had never expressed his desire for another son. In 1983, I talked to Wayne about possibly adopting a Native American boy. It seemed to me to be a good solution for us having a son. I continued to pray about adoption, and I had shared my desire with my mom and dad.

BUT GOD sent my dad to me to talk about my desire for an adopted son. He pointed out to me that only God's will should be done. Dad spoke to me about Abraham and Sarah, and how they had not had a child like God had promised them. Sarah had told Abraham "the Lord has not allowed me to have children, so sleep with my slave, Hagar. Maybe she can have a son…" (Genesis 16:2, ERV). Abraham did what Sarah said even though this was according to their flesh, and not by the Spirit of God. Hagar became pregnant and named the son Ishmael. Then Sarah became pregnant by Abraham and the Holy Spirit, and had a son named Isaac. Ishmael and Hagar made fun of Isaac, and Sarah became angry. Sarah turned to Abraham, and demanded, "Get rid of that slave woman and her son. He is not going to share the inheritance with my son, Isaac. I won't have it!" (Genesis 21:10) God told Abraham to do whatever Sarah said.

My dad warned me not to adopt a son based upon my fleshly desire, or I would be producing an Ishmael. I knew this was the Word of the Lord. I was suddenly frightened and knew I could not go against the will of God. I prayed for God's will to be done, and I cried out to God to either give me peace without a son or give me a son. I read and prayed Hannah's prayer for a son in 1 Samuel 1:10-18, "O Lord of Heaven's Armies, If You will look upon my sorrow and answer my prayer, and give me a son, then I will give him back to You. He will be Yours for his entire lifetime...."

I promised God if He would give me a son I would dedicate him to the Lord, and I would name him Jonathan, which means God's gracious gift. I also claimed Acts 10:34, "God is no respecter of persons." Whatever He did for Hannah, He would also do for me.

I continued praying and speaking God's Word daily. I knew I had to desire God more than anything in my life, even more than my own will and desire. He was my God, my King, my Savior, my everything!

May of 1983, I found out that I was pregnant again. One part of me was excited, and another part of me was concerned. Due to the fact I was 35 years old, the doctor felt like I should have an amniocentesis in case there were any problems with the baby. The amniocentesis entailed having a long needle penetrate the amniotic sack and drawing out some fluid. The fluid would determine if there was anything wrong with the baby, and it also told what sex the baby was.

A week after I had the amniocentesis procedure, I had a doctor's appointment. Wayne was not able to go with me. The doctor examined me and told me the results of the test which showed the baby was healthy, for which I was very grateful. He wanted to know if I wanted him to tell me the sex of the baby. I said no because I wanted Wayne to be with me when I learned the gender of the baby. I prayed all the way home from Tulsa for God's peace to be upon me.

> "Be anxious for nothing, but in everything by prayer and supplication, with thanksgiving, let your requests be made known to God; and the peace of God, which passeth all understanding, shall keep your hearts and minds through Christ Jesus."
> Philippians 4:6-7

When I rounded the corner to our house, I saw Wayne in the front yard practicing his golf swing. I thought that was strange for him to be at home in the middle of the day. When we walked into the house, I went to our bedroom to change clothes. Wayne followed me into the bedroom, and I told him about my doctor's visit. I told him that I told the doctor I didn't want to know the gender of the baby until he could be with me. Wayne then told me that he had called the doctor's office and asked about the results of the test. My heart started beating so fast, and he said, 'IT'S A BOY!" We held each other close as we cried and laughed and praised the Lord! God heard my prayers and answered!

> "For this boy I prayed, and the Lord has given me my petition which I asked of Him."
> 1 Samuel 1:27

We decided not to tell anyone that we were having a boy; we wanted it to be a big surprise. Our daughter Jennifer, who was nine years old, had said throughout my pregnancy that she was sure the baby was going to be a boy. I thought of the scripture in Matthew 18:19, "Again I say unto you, that if two of you shall agree on earth as touching anything that they shall ask, it shall be done for them of my Father who is in Heaven."

On February 28, 1984, Jonathan was born! We decided to give him my dad's name as his middle name, and a third name that we liked. His birth certificate reads, Jonathan Richard Tanner Buck. Jonathan means 'God's gracious gift'. Jonathan surely was a gift from God to our whole family. Wayne called the school and asked to talk to three of our four girls on speaker phone. The principal had them come into his office. Our girls were so excited to hear they had a brother! Jennifer said, "I knew it was a boy!" Wayne brought the girls to the hospital to see me, and to meet their new brother. It was a time of great rejoicing, laughter, and giving thanks unto God.

When we got home from the hospital, my mom and dad, and other family members came over to see this little answer to prayer. My dad was so proud that we had selected his name, Richard, for Jonathan's middle name. Plus, Jonathan had reddish auburn hair like my dad and me.

I was grateful that my dad loved me enough to give me the word of the Lord and stop me from making a terrible mistake in the flesh. BUT GOD had a plan all along, and He fulfilled my heart's desire! "Delight yourself in the Lord and He will give you the desires of your heart" (Psalm 37:4, NASB).

4
Whitney's Bicycle Accident

Whitney is our third daughter. As a child and even in adulthood she has been reserved. She didn't like doing anything that drew attention to herself. She was a very pleasant child and didn't like to argue with her siblings or friends. She was a very pretty child with dark brown hair and eyes. She looked a lot like my mom when she was young. Whitney had a very special friend from church, Tara, whom Whitney had over to the house often. They both loved riding their bicycles. One day when Whitney was 10 years old Tara came over and they decided to ride their bikes up a small hill to play at The Grant Foreman Elementary School playground. It was summertime so no one else was there. After playing awhile they headed back home to our house on their bikes.

As Tara and Whitney pedaled their bikes on the street, they then started down the hill. They didn't realize the downward pull of their bikes would require less speed. They both applied their brakes, but Whitney's bike was not slowing, and at the bottom of the hill was a sharp right turn. Since Whitney's brakes weren't holding, she was unable to guide the bike to the right. Over and into a deep ditch she flew bike and all. She was screaming and crying on impact. Tara was terrified for her friend and ran up the hill to the house of a church friend of ours for help.

Kay was able to get Whitney and bring her to her house. She called us immediately, I called Wayne at work, and we drove to get Whitney. Kay took care of Tara and made sure she got home. Kay also called the church for prayer for Whitney. Tara was terrified for her friend.

We immediately took Whitney to the Pediatrician's office. I was praying over Whitney who had road rash, and two cuts on her face. When the doctor looked in her ears he saw blood. He turned to us and said he was sure she had a fractured skull and possibly brain bleeding. BUT GOD had a different plan for Whitney! The doctor told us to take her to the Emergency Room right away.

We had a big van, and we laid Whitney back in the seat, so she was semi-lying down. Wayne drove and I sat beside Whitney speaking and declaring every scripture I could think of and binding every evil force that was set against Whitney. I loosed the healing and restorative power of the blood and stripes of Jesus. "He was wounded for our transgressions, He was bruised for our iniquities, the chastisement of our peace was upon Him, and by His stripes we are healed" (Isaiah 53:5). I knew we had to keep Whitney awake so I asked her to say every scripture after me. I knew we were in a spiritual battle and the only way to win was with the Word of God.

When we arrived at the hospital Wayne carried Whitney into the Emergency Room, where our doctor had notified them that we were coming. They immediately took Whitney to have an MRI and other tests done. When she returned to her room, the doctor stitched up the cuts over her lip and eyebrow and cleaned the areas of road rash on her face.

Finally, after everyone read the MRI and other tests the doctor gave us the report. He said Whitney had a mild concussion, but there was no skull fracture and no brain bleeding. She was ordered to rest for several days. Hallelujah!! To God Almighty be all the glory, honor, and praise!

"But You, oh Lord, art a shield for me; the glory and the lifter of my head"
Psalms 3:3

5
God's Grace for Wayne

My husband, Wayne, really enjoys playing golf, though he only gets to play once in a while in the summer. One day at noon he decided to go out to the Muskogee Country Club and practice his irons. He had hit multiple balls and was enjoying his time outside. He set another ball down and made his calculated back swing with a power-driven downswing. As he hit the ball with his 8 iron, suddenly the ball exploded! The debris and inner ball forcefully smashed into his left eye knocking him to his knees. He immediately cried out to God for help!

Wayne was unable to see out of either eye. As he waited to catch his breath, he was soon able to see partially out of his right eye and then got to his feet. He slowly walked over to the golf cart and got inside. Wayne carefully drove the cart back to the club house, and walked in. He told the Pro who was there what had happened, and he felt he could drive himself to the eye doctor's office. When the optometrist examined Wayne's eye she referred him immediately to the Ophthalmologist. Wayne drove to the doctor's office which was on the other side of town. Still there was no vision in his left eye. He never thought to call me because I was working, and he didn't want me to be upset. He was thoughtful, but not practical.

When the ophthalmologist examined Wayne's left eye, he stated that there was a lot of inflammation and some bleeding from the impact of the ball. He put drops in his eye and ordered him to stay in a recliner at a 45-degree angle for 5 days and to take two different prescription drops in his eye. His right eye showed no damage.

When I got home from teaching at school that day, I was shocked to see Wayne sitting in his recliner with a black and blue, very swollen left eye! He had been holding a frozen bag of corn gently to his eye to help reduce the swelling. He described in detail what all had happened to him. He also told me what the doctor prescribed for his eye to heal, and to prevent a detached retina, or bleeding in the eye. I prayed for Wayne immediately, asking the Lord to heal and restore his eye, and grant him his full vision. Our dependence now was totally on God.

It was very difficult for Wayne to sit, and sleep in the recliner for 5 days. He wanted to be at work, and out-and-about, but this was a very critical time of healing, and he just couldn't take any short cuts. The only thing he could get up for was to go to the bathroom. He wasn't allowed to take showers. He was only allowed to take sponge baths. The doctor was emphatic that Wayne wasn't allowed to bend over at all! Five days seemed like an exceedingly long time, BUT GOD's grace helped us through.

By the 6th day, Wayne's eye looked so much better, except for a few broken vessels. He was able to see again with full clarity! He visited the doctor again, and he said all looked well, but to continue to be mildly cautious. We gave praise and thanksgiving to our God for all that he had done in this frightening situation!

Many people said Wayne was a lucky man because he could have lost his eye and his vision. BUT GOD's Word says, "I sought the Lord and

He heard me, and delivered me from all my fears" (Psalms 34:4, KJV). God heard Wayne's initial cry for help, and He honored our daily seeking Him, and declaring His healing Word. Our hearts were in awe of our all-powerful God!

6
Keithe's Bump in the Road

In 1989, my oldest sister, Keithe, was diagnosed with stage 4 breast cancer. She was a nurse at a hospital in Oldsmar, Florida. When she was reaching to get something from a high shelf, she felt a pull and a restriction under her right arm. When she examined herself, she felt a rather large knot. She was almost certain what that meant. Keithe made an appointment with her Gynecologist, and she immediately sent Keithe for an ultrasound of her right breast. All tests showed she had stage 4 cancer of the breast. Keithe called our mom and dad and told them her diagnosis. Then our parents told the three of us sisters. It was hard to hear because there was so much fear connected to the word cancer. But as a family we knew that prayer and trust in God was the only way she would have a chance to live. "A prayer offered in faith will heal the sick, and the Lord will make you well." (James 5:15, NLT) When I talked to her on the phone she said, "It's only a bump in the road of my life."

She was sent to a surgeon who specialized in Mastectomies. The surgeon highly recommended a full Mastectomy since it was stage 4 cancer. Keithe had the surgery and was then scheduled for chemo and radiation. The surgery was difficult, and now she had to endure the chemo and radiation. Keithe was being treated by a doctor who had been trained by John Hopkins. She was given large doses of extraordinarily strong chemo; much stronger than they use now. She lost all of her beautiful auburn hair and was very sick from the treatments. I remember talking to her on the phone, and we both would cry because of all that she was going through. Keithe had always been a strong person; and now she was totally out of control, weak, and vulnerable. BUT GOD had a plan to heal and restore her.

The doctor decided to put Keithe in the hospital and do a bone marrow transplant. They withdrew her bone marrow from her hip, which was a very painful procedure, and it had a nauseating smell.

I remember her telling me how they gave her an orange to suck on and to smell during the procedure. The bone marrow was then sent to a special lab that cleaned it of all cancer cells. Then they injected the bone marrow back into her bones, which was also very painful, and nauseating to smell.

After a couple of weeks in the hospital they did some tests, and it showed the bone marrow transplant was working! Things were turning around. She was the first person in the United States in which this procedure was successful. For the next several months Keithe continued to improve, and tests finally showed she was cancer free!

"For I will restore health to you, and heal you of your wounds, says the Lord"
Jeremiah 30:17, NKJV

There's an old song that says, "Look what the Lord has done! He healed my body, He touched my mind, He saved me just in time!" This was Keithe's victory song!

7
Andrea and Heather's Car Accident

A week after our youngest daughter, Andrea's 10th birthday, I asked our oldest daughter, Heather, to go pick her up at soccer practice. I normally would have gone myself, but I was dealing with a situation with another daughter. I told Heather that she was not to drive unless Andrea had her seat belt and shoulder harness on, because Andrea had recently been taking off her shoulder harness in the car. The time had changed to Standard Time the Sunday before so it was getting dark an hour earlier.

Heather told me later that Andrea got in the car, and Heather had to remind her to 'buckle up'. Andrea argued with Heather, but Heather insisted she wouldn't go until Andrea had her full seat belt on. Andrea put on her full seat belt, and Heather proceeded to drive. However, Andrea laid her seat back and removed the shoulder harness strap.

Heather pulled out onto Highway 64 going north. Soon after that a car with 2 teenage girls going south turned right in front of Heather causing Heather to hit the passenger side of the front seat. Both cars then spun around hitting 2 other cars.

I received a phone call from a lady who was very panicky telling me my two girls were in a severe car accident, and the police were having to use the Jaws of Life to get them out of the car. I immediately called Wayne at work and told him where the accident happened, and to meet me there. I told my one daughter, Jennifer, to take care of Whitney and Jonathan.

I ran to my van and was screaming at the devil to take his hands off of my girls, and that "no weapon formed against them shall prosper!" (Isaiah 54:17) I was desperate for God's intervention! I was crying and speaking every scripture I could think of; "God gives His angels charge over you, to keep you in all your ways. In their hands they shall bear you up lest you dash your foot against a stone" (Psalm

91:11-12). Wild imaginings were bombarding my mind! Were they going to die, would they be crippled, did they have brain trauma? I started screaming "NO" to the devil and fear! I shouted "I am strong and courageous. I will NOT be afraid or terrified because of what's happened, for the Lord my God goes with me and my daughters: He will never leave us or forsake us! (Deuteronomy 31:6).

When I arrived at the site of the accident the EMS attendants were loading Heather, and Andrea into the ambulance. Andrea was covered in blood, and her top front teeth had been knocked out. Heather's eyes were swollen almost shut and turning black. Heather had her full seat belt on yet due to her short stature she slammed her head on the steering wheel, causing her eyes to swell. She had extremely severe seat belt bruising which was so very painful for her to sit or lay down.

Wayne and I met the ambulance at the hospital emergency room. We were in shock and desperate to know the diagnosis. The doctor came out, and said Heather had the worst seat belt bruising he'd ever seen, and a possible concussion. He said Andrea had a shattered jaw on both sides, as well as a subarachnoid hemorrhage in the brain. We were stunned.

When we saw Andrea she was nauseated, vomiting, and blood was draining down the back of her throat. Heather was in severe pain, and her eyes were swollen almost shut, and looked like black golf balls. However, the hospital dismissed her to our dismay.

Wayne and I helped Heather into Wayne's Mustang, but it wasn't easy due to the severe seat belt and sternum bruising. It was excruciatingly painful for her. Wayne drove her home and helped get her settled in the recliner. She wasn't able to lay down so she sat in the recliner slightly reclined with the foot rest up to sleep. Wayne had to make sure our other 3 children, Jennifer, Whitney, and Jonathan, were taken care of, and gotten off to school the next day. Andrea, by the grace of God, was in good spirits. The ambulance workers gave her a stuffed animal to hold onto. Finally, Andrea was put in a room in ICU where they allowed me to stay with her all night.

The first night in ICU Andrea would sleep but would thrash with her head and shoulders jerking up and down. The nurse said it was caused by the brain injury. I was awake all night praying in the

Spirit and holding Andrea's hand. I was declaring healing, for the brain swelling to go down, for the bleeding to stop in the brain, and total restoration for Andrea. It felt like a very dark time during that first night, BUT GOD was with us. I knew and declared His promises. "Be strong and courageous. Do not be afraid or terrified because of this, for the Lord our God goes with [us]; He will never leave [us] or forsake [us]" (Deuteronomy 31:6). I made God's Word personal for us.

I could feel His grace though fear was trying to tell me Andrea would never be the same again. I knew God had a better plan for Andrea. We named her Andrea because it means "Strong woman of God". I determined no devil in hell was going to stop the plan of God for Andrea! I praised God and spoke His healing promises over Andrea throughout the night. "[Andrea] shall not die but live to declare the glorious works of the Lord" (Psalms 118:17). "Heal [Andrea and Heather] oh Lord, and they shall be healed, save them and they shall be saved, for You are our praise" (Jeremiah 17:14). "Behold God will bring health and healing. He will heal Andrea and Heather and reveal to them the abundance of peace and truth" (Jeremiah 33:6).

The next day Andrea was doing better. The jerking and thrashing had ceased, and most of the bleeding in the brain had stopped. A Maxillofacial Surgeon came in and said they were doing more x-rays. The x-rays showed the extent of the shattered jaw. He recommended that Andrea be transferred to Children's Hospital in Oklahoma City, and for this well-known Maxillofacial Surgeon, Dr. Markowitz, to do the surgery to rebuild Andrea's jaw.

Two days later Andrea was placed in a regular hospital room. She had improved greatly and had a lot of visitors. Her sisters and brother were so happy to be able to finally visit her. Our Pastors from our Tulsa church came down and prayed for Andrea and went to our house to pray for Heather. I felt bad because there wasn't much any of us could do for Heather. She needed time to heal. Andrea's classmates made a banner for her with drawings and get-well messages on it. Her classmates also wrote get-well notes, and cards to Andrea. Churches throughout Muskogee were praying for Andrea and Heather. All of this helped Andrea, but the most help came from the Holy Spirit who poured out God's abundant grace upon Andrea, Heather, and me. "My grace is all you need. My power and mercy work best in weakness" (2 Corinthians 12:9, NLT).

On the fourth day Andrea was transported by ambulance to Children's Hospital in Oklahoma City, Oklahoma. Wayne and I followed. After they got Andrea settled, Dr. Markowitz came in and introduced himself, and talked to us about the detailed surgery he would be performing on Andrea. He stated that in four months we could try to have dental implants for Andrea's top front teeth.

The next day Andrea had surgery to rebuild her jaw. It took over 6 hours. Waiting was very difficult for me, BUT GOD's presence was there to encourage me. "He sent His Word and healed [Andrea] and delivered [her] from this destruction" (Psalm 107:20).

Finally, Dr. Markowitz came out and said all went well. He was able to reconstruct the jaw and used screws to help hold pieces together. Her mouth was wired shut temporarily. She was already on a liquid diet so that wasn't a problem. Andrea had a difficult time coming out of the anesthesia. She wept and wept, and they had to give her meds to calm her down. She finally calmed down, and I was able to give her a thin milk shake. I stayed with Andrea for the next two weeks while she recovered. "God will watch over His Word to perform it" (Jeremiah 1:12).

Wayne had to be at home for work, tending to Heather, cooking, managing the other kids, and their schoolwork, and doing laundry. We talked often during the day and at night. Wayne drove to Oklahoma City to the hospital 2 days a week. It was over a two-hour drive one way from Muskogee. We all had to be strong during this time. "Finally, be strong in the Lord, and the power of His might. Put on the whole armour of God, that ye may be able to stand against the wiles of the devil" (Ephesians 6:10-11, KJV). We were so grateful to all our friends and family who helped with our children so Wayne could come to the hospital.

It was a time of healing for Andrea, and a time of us growing closer. There were days when Andrea was frustrated, and just wanted to go home, and days when she was even fearful of going back to school; what the kids would say, and how would they treat her. I would read Andrea Bible stories, and we'd talk about God being a good God, and a healing God. She asked why God let the accident happen. I explained to her that it wasn't God's will, but the girl driving the car wasn't driving safely, and that Andrea hadn't obeyed and kept her shoulder harness on. I explained we all make choices and mistakes, and sometimes our choices or other's choices cause harm, **BUT GOD** had saved Heather and her, and given Andrea amazing doctors, surgeons, and nurses to help her recover. Even to the point that the main attending nurse for Andrea was named Andrea Paige Buck just like our Andrea's full name. She had just gotten married in May, which gave her the last name of Buck. We knew this was a sign from God that He was taking care of Andrea. "This is the Lord's sign to you that the Lord will do what he has promised" (Isaiah 38:7, NIV).

There were days of laughter and playing cards, and days of solemnness. Then came the day when Dr. Markowitz came in and said he was discharging Andrea. We were told to come back in 2 weeks when he would unwire her jaw. Andrea was so excited! Dr. Markowitz gave her 3 bags of candy from his 3 children who went trick-or-treating for Andrea since she was in the hospital. Of course, he told her the candy had to wait for at least another month. What a thoughtful thing for those kids to do for Andrea! The doctor instructed us to keep Andrea home for at least another 2 weeks.

At home Andrea's teacher, Mrs. Stotts, visited a couple times a week, and brought homework for her to work on. She always brought 'get well' papers with drawings on them for Andrea from her fourth grade classmates. This always raised Andrea's spirit. A couple of days before Andrea went back to school I asked if she would be willing to go with me to an assembly at one of the schools where I was a Speech-Language Pathologist. I was asked to give a talk on 'Seat Belt Safety'. I thought Andrea might want to talk to some of the kids about her experience. She agreed.

As I gave students a verbal picture of what Andrea and Heather had experienced in their car accident, the children were very attentive. When given time for questions the children asked Andrea how it felt to be in an accident. Andrea stated it happened so fast when the teenager turned in front of their car that she didn't have time to think about what was happening. But she did say it was scary, and it hurt for a long time. She did tell them that the car was spinning and hitting other cars. She told them she had removed her shoulder harness, and her top teeth were knocked out from hitting the gear shift, and her jaw and head had hit the dash and gear shift. I told the children that God had a different plan for Andrea, and He had saved her and Heather from death. I told them what the devil meant for bad God was turning for good by telling other kids about seat belt safety. The kids saw Andrea's cuts and bruises, and they could see her jaw was still bruised and swollen. It was obvious that the children were impacted by seeing and talking to Andrea. Andrea was so brave to do this. What satan meant for evil, God turned to good (Genesis 50:20).

When Andrea returned to school she struggled. The brain trauma in the frontal lobe of the brain affected her emotions. She exhibited increased irritation and anger which seemed to appear for no good reason. Trauma often expresses itself in anger. Andrea stated she didn't know why she felt irritated and angry. Yet we could see that the irritation and anger wasn't really targeted at what someone said or did, but rather it was coming from the anger in her heart toward what she had experienced, and gone through.

We tried to get her to talk about what had happened to her, but she just didn't want to talk. We tried counseling, but she wouldn't talk there either. I felt God was showing me that Andrea was also mad at herself for taking off the shoulder harness, but she didn't want to admit this. We continued to pray God's Word over her mind, emotions, and spirit day and night. "I am the Lord who heals you" (Exodus 15:26). "I will restore you to health, and heal your wounds' declares the Lord" (Jeremiah 30:17). "He heals the broken hearted, and binds up their wounds" (Psalm 147:3).

Dr. Markowitz tried to put dental implants in for Andrea's front teeth, but her bone would not accept the posts. She ended up having a flipper plate. She gained a little more confidence once she had her front teeth back. She had lost her child-like innocence because of the accident and all she went through. Now she had to figure out how to be happy, and appreciative of God saving her life. God continued to work with Andrea for years to come. I believe that inner healing sometimes takes a lifetime depending on how deep it goes, but as we continue to give those hurts and memories to God He is faithful to complete the healing.

8
God's Mercy and Grace for Andrea

Andrea is our fourth daughter who has always been strong-willed. She started a bit shy and would hide behind me when greeting people at church. She then grew to be more independent and didn't like following instructions. She wanted to do things her way, which wasn't always beneficial for her life. When she was fifteen years old, she went to a neighbor boy's house, of whom she was told to stay away from. I was working in summer school, and the boy's parents were at work. He asked Andrea to come over to watch a movie. They started to watch the movie, but then the boy attacked Andrea, even though she told him "No" several times. She tried to push him away, but unfortunately he assaulted her.

When I returned home that day, I could tell Andrea was acting withdrawn. Following up on my intuition I asked her if anything was wrong. She replied, no. However, after a couple of months, she came to us and told us she was pregnant, and what had happened. We were devastated for her. We called the District Attorney and had a meeting with him about pressing charges against the boy. When the D.A. explained that it would be her word against his and that his lawyer would make her out to be a "slut" Andrea decided against filing charges.

> *"Be strong and courageous, do not be afraid or tremble at them, for the Lord your God is the one who goes with you. He will not fail you or forsake you."*
> *Deuteronomy 31:6*

It was a very difficult time in Andrea's and our lives. We knew we could not raise a baby. Both Wayne and I worked full-time, and I worked after school providing home health services for speech therapy. We still had Andrea and Jonathan at home and lots of bills. Andrea had to finish school to have any kind of a future.

After a lot of searching and prayer, we took Andrea to Hannah's House of Prayer, which was a home for unwed mothers. It was run by Higher Dimensions Church in Tulsa, Oklahoma. They ministered to the girls daily and helped them prepare for employment, taught them money management and other life skills. They also had them attending in-house school. They gave them the choice of adoption for their babies. They had notebooks about families who wanted to adopt. There were pictures, family backgrounds, and heartfelt letters of their desires to adopt. Andrea decided to place her child up for adoption.

Throughout the months of her pregnancy, Andrea frequently said, "I just want my life back." We wanted that for her too. She would be about sixteen and a half when she would give birth. We knew things in her life would never be the same, but we wanted it to be as close to normal as possible.

During Andrea's last month of pregnancy, she chose a family from Plano, Texas. They could not have their own children, and they had adopted two children previously. Everything about them drew Andrea to them. They were strong Christians, the father had a great job, and they liked to travel as a family. Andrea asked our opinions, and we supported her. This was a very heart wrenching situation Andrea was in, BUT GOD had a plan.

When we had the interview with the adoptive parents it was obvious that Andrea had picked the right family. Their personalities, love of Jesus, and all-around life principles seemed to align with what Andrea, and we believed. God was working in this difficult situation. Andrea was in the hospital for several days after giving birth to her son because he had jaundice. Andrea nursed him and held him close during those days. We took many pictures of him for her album.

Then the day came for her to hand her baby over to the adoptive parents. There are few things that are as painful as giving your child up for adoption though you know it's the right and the best thing to do for the child's sake. "There is no greater love than to lay down one's life for one's friends" (John 15:13, NLT). I believe you can substitute the word "another" for "friend." The emotional pain was outrageous for Andrea, and for us.

Two days later, our church had a special ceremony for blessing Andrea, the baby, and the adoptive parents. It helped in many ways. Proverbs 17:6, states that "Grandchildren are the crowning glory of the aged; parents are the pride of their children." Psalms 127:3, states that "Children are a gift from the LORD; they are a reward from him."

For the next month, Andrea cried a lot, and so did we. She had a hard time sitting at home to recover, so when she was ready, we went back to the private Christian school she had been attending. However, they said their guidelines forbid a girl from attending if she has had a baby. Andrea was distraught. So, we prayed every day for guidance. Then we decided to go before the school board and ask for mercy, and grace for Andrea to be able to attend. We had a letter from our pastor in Tulsa that asked for forgiveness and abundant grace and favor for Andrea due to this heart wrenching situation. All the school board members were friends of ours, but the rules were set for a reason, and we were asking them to consider the intensity, and gravity of this situation. We needed God's favor with the board.

"So you will find favor and good esteem in the sight of God and man."
Proverbs 3:4, NKJV

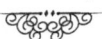

I was very emotional and knew I would not be of any help, so Wayne and Andrea went to the school board hearing. As they stood before the school board they were asked questions. They wanted to know why we hadn't reported the rape and had the District Attorney file charges against the boy. Wayne explained that we did, but the trauma of a "she said, he said" trial would not have brought justice. They also asked if Andrea wanted to come back to school and why. She said she did because she wanted to continue her education and be with friends. She didn't talk much because she was still suffering from the trauma of rape, and the heartbreak from placing her baby up for adoption. After the hearing, the board said they would get in touch with us about their decision.

Later that night we received a phone call from the President of the school board stating Andrea could be reinstated as a student at the school. WOW! God had granted Andrea His favor, grace, and mercy. This was such a relief for us and for Andrea; we praised God and thanked Him for moving on the hearts of the school board members.

The next couple of years were difficult for Andrea. We continued to take her to counseling in Tulsa, but it didn't seem to help. She had a very angry, hostile attitude toward everyone. She thought she would be able to "get her life back," but her trauma robbed her of her youth. It was like her life was shortened. Instead of being a young innocent teenager discovering age-appropriate things, now she had to figure out how to live with the torment that trauma brings. However, even with all of these issues, Andrea was able to graduate from high school and went on to get her associate's degree in college.

When she moved out to continue her college studies, we thought she had adjusted and moved on, and was happy, but she was still troubled. We didn't know what to do, so we continued to do what we always did, pray. Annually Andrea would get letters and pictures of her son from the adoptive parents, and we would send money for birthdays, and Christmas. We continue to do this to this very day.

Her son is now 24 years old, and he has had every privilege, and great experiences a child could have. He and his family have traveled to many places, and he's experienced things that we nor Andrea could've ever given him. His adoptive parents were very loving people. He is highly creative, and a lover of life. He and Andrea have connected several times on the internet though they have not met, that is still our prayer for them and for us. God has shown He is with us no matter the situation if we will follow and trust Him. The only way for pain to be healed is through the Holy Spirit one layer at a time as we surrender. "The Lord is near to the brokenhearted and saves those who are crushed in spirit" (Psalm 34:18).

9
Wayne's Heart

One Sunday morning our family drove to church from Muskogee to Tulsa as was our typical Sunday. Wayne and I were on the worship team where Wayne played guitar and we both sang. The message was motivating, and we really enjoyed our church family. It was a warm Fall day. Wayne was driving Andrea, Jonathan, and me home where we planned to fix lunch. Wayne's 60's band had a gig that evening at a prison near Oklahoma City. So, as we were traveling down the expressway, Wayne and I were discussing his gig when suddenly he sighed and fell forward unconscious on the steering wheel. I kept yelling Wayne's name and I was praying loudly to God declaring His Word! "No weapon formed against [Wayne] shall prosper" (Isaiah 54:17).

Andrea was screaming and crying. I yelled at her to call 911 on her cell phone. Jonathan jumped up from the back seat, and pulled Wayne off the steering wheel so that I could steer the car to the side of the road. I yelled at Andrea again to call 911! She finally did, and I was able to stretch my leg over and pressed the brake so we could stop and shift the gear into park. As this was happening Wayne woke up and said "No don't call 911. I'm fine." He and I argued for a minute and Wayne got his way. Andrea told them he was fine now. She stopped crying, and Jonathan sat back down. I was shaking and tearful. BUT GOD heard my prayers and prevented what could 've been a terrible tragedy.

Wayne and I switched seats because I insisted on driving. I told him we were going to the hospital in Muskogee. He was not happy about that! He kept saying he had to go with the band, but I insisted that we seek medical attention to find out what had caused this sudden blackout. He finally submitted to common sense. He called the band leader and told them what had happened and said he wouldn't be able to go with them to the prison.

When we arrived at the ER in Muskogee, they took him right into a room. They called his heart doctor and did multiple tests. They finally let him go home, but he was to see the heart doctor the next day. The doctor was puzzled and ordered several more tests. Wayne wasn't feeling bad, but this incident was frightening. The tests all came back good, **BUT GOD** already knew what the problem was. The doctor ordered Wayne to wear a heart monitor that would record any irregular heartbeat Wayne would feel, and then he had to push the button.

Wayne wore the monitor almost all of November and he hadn't had any real problem. We had been praying for Wayne and asking God to reveal what was wrong and show it to the doctor. Our church was also praying for Wayne to be healed or for the problem to be revealed to the doctor. Then on Thanksgiving Day after we had eaten, Wayne went into the garage to get some ice from the freezer when suddenly he started to lose consciousness! Andrea was at the kitchen door talking to Wayne when she suddenly saw him passing out. Andrea jumped over two steps, and pushed the button on the machine, and helped her dad lay down. Andrea yelled for me, and I rushed to the garage. By that time Wayne was awake and confused. About 10 minutes later we received a call from the hospital that Wayne's heart had stopped, and for him to come immediately to the hospital.

When we arrived at the hospital, they quickly took him into a room, and they had a surgeon there waiting for him. The surgeon said he needed a Pacemaker because he had Atrial Fibrillation. Atrial Fibrillation is an irregular heartbeat; Wayne's heart would beat irregularly and skip beats and then not beat again. The surgeon put the Pacemaker in Wayne's chest, and they kept him overnight to make sure all was well. Wayne didn't have any more situations of sudden passing out due to Atrial Fibrillation. Three years later Wayne had an Ablation where they go in and burn the nerves that are causing the heart to race from the Atrial Fibrillation. He's had 3 other Ablations, but he's lived a very full life.

We know that Wayne will not die from heart problems, because Ken Clement, a well-known and documented prophet of God, called Wayne out by name at a meeting, and prophesied that Wayne would not die from heart problems, and he would live a long life. The Bible says, "...Believe in the Lord your God, and you shall be established; believe His prophets, and you shall prosper" (2 Chronicles 20:20b). "But the Lord is faithful, and He will strengthen you and protect you from the evil one" (Lamentations 3:22-23).

We're so very grateful to God that He always hears our prayers, and the petitions of His saints. Wayne continues to play bass guitar with a rock 'n roll band, and for our church worship team. He continues to work as an Insurance Agent at the age of 79. God is good all the time; all the time my God is good!

10
Wayne's Faith Challenge

*E*veryone encounters some kind of challenges in their lives whether it's financial, physical, emotional, or spiritual. Then there are those challenges that are all four. In 2010, Wayne began having a very sharp pain in his left shoulder ball joint with some tingling and numbness in his arm and fingers. Wayne doesn't usually complain, but this pain had gotten worse. For about 3-4 weeks Wayne was telling me how bad this pain was, and I kept telling him to go the doctor. By the time he finally went to the doctor the pain in his shoulder and numbness in his fingers had gotten much worse.

The doctor wasn't sure what the pain was or what was causing it, so he sent him to another doctor who recommended he go to a specialist.

The specialist did an x-ray of Wayne's shoulder and neck. When he came back into the room, he showed us the x-ray and pointed out two masses. One was on the bottom of the brain stem, and another was encapsulated at the top of the spinal cord. Immediately we looked at each other and said, "We refuse this in Jesus' name!" The doctor continued to explain that Wayne needed an MRI. Wayne explained he had a pacemaker and wasn't able to get an MRI. The doctor referred him to a specialist/researcher who recently was performing MRIs on patients who had pacemakers.

As soon as we got into the car we prayed and rebuked the tumors in Wayne's brain, and declared God's Word that says by the blood and stripes of Jesus we are healed! "He personally carried our sins in his body on the cross so that we can be dead to sin and live for what is right. By His wounds you are healed" (1 Peter 2:24, NLT).

All kinds of worry and fear were attacking our thoughts, and yet we knew God's Word was true! Every day we had to declare God's Word into the heavenlies and into the natural. We were in a war for Wayne's health. "For the weapons of our warfare are not carnal, but mighty to the pulling down of strong holds; casting down imaginations, and every high thing that exalteth itself against the knowledge of God, and bring into captivity every thought to the obedience of Christ" (2 Corinthians 10:4-5, KJV).

Wayne was able to have the MRI which clearly showed 2 brain tumors. In our prayers we declared these tumors had no right to exist in Wayne's brain, and they had to go! We declared that Wayne's body, including his brain, was the temple of the Holy Spirit, and no evil or sick thing had a right to stay. "Do you not know that your bodies are temples of the Holy Spirit, who is in you, whom you have received from God? You are not your own; you were bought at a price. Therefore honor God with your bodies" (1 Corinthians 6:19-20, NIV). Either way God was going to do an instant miraculous healing, or a miraculous healing through surgery. This was our confession, and our belief.

Soon after the MRI, our doctor referred us to a well-known brain surgeon in Tulsa, Oklahoma, Dr. Daniel Boedeker. He was truly kind, and explained the placement of the tumors, and what he would have to do to remove them. It sounded so scary, BUT GOD already had a plan! Our part in God's plan was to trust Him, seek Him in prayer, and to declare and decree His promises into Heaven and in this earth.

During our days of prayer Wayne and I both felt that we were to be incredibly careful with whom we shared our situation. We felt the Holy Spirit was telling us that fear and negative words would work against God's plan and us. We made the extremely hard decision to not tell our five children until right before the surgery. We had shared the situation with our pastors, and a select few that we knew would pray for us with strong faith in God. I also told my three sisters because they had gone through some rough trials and had strong faith in praying.

"These trials are only to assess your faith, to see whether or not it is strong and pure. It is being tested as fire tests gold and purifies it—and your faith is far more precious to God than mere gold; so if your faith remains strong after being tried in the test tube of fiery trial, it will bring you much praise and glory and honor on the day of His return" (1Peter 1:7-9, TLB).

My oldest sister, Keithe, flew in from Florida to be with me during the surgery and to help afterward. She was a certified nurse. Many years before her husband had to have a similar surgery, and I had flown to be with her as a support. Two days before Wayne's surgery we told our five children about the surgery. Three of them were angry with us and said they deserved to know before this. The other two were more understanding. We did what we believed the Holy Spirit instructed us to do in order to prevent negative, fearful words spoken out against their dad.

The day of the surgery Wayne, Keithe, and I arrived at the hospital at about 5:30 a.m. We had driven an hour from our home in Muskogee to Tulsa. We were surprised when we arrived that our dear friend, Jo Dee, was there to pray over Wayne. She has an amazing voice, and as we declared the powerful healing Word of God she began to sing "We are Standing on Holy Ground." As we all joined in singing, the presence of the Holy Spirit rushed into the room. We modulated the song, and an even stronger presence of God came into the room. Down the hall from Wayne's room was a nurse who heard our full out singing with harmonies to God. She came running down the hallway and into the room crying and said, "I've got to have this!" We continued to pray and lay hands on her to which her knees began to buckle. We prayed in the Spirit over her until the doctor came into the room, and she left with such a joy. The presence of the Lord continued in the room.

The doctor explained about the procedures, and how he would remove the golf ball size tumor in the bottom of the brain stem, and the other thumb size tumor that was encapsulated at the top of the spinal cord. He stated it would be a 10–12-hour surgery. He also explained there was a chance of some paralysis. When he said this all four of us were saying softly, 'NO!' "No weapon formed against 'Wayne" shall prosper" (Isaiah 54:17, ASV).

When He finished explaining we asked if we could pray for him which we did. We prayed and declared that his hands would be God's hands today in this surgery, and everything he did would be directed by God for the well-being of Wayne. When the doctor left the room, we all prayed that Wayne would come through the surgery with no side effects, and that he would recover fully and completely. I declared, "You will not die but live and declare the (glorious) works of the Lord!" (Psalm 118:17, NKJV) With that I kissed Wayne, and the nurse came in to take him into surgery.

My sister Keithe, Jo Dee, and I each took a deep breath, and sighed. Now the long wait began. Jo Dee had to leave to go to work, so we all hugged, and she said she'd be interceding while she was at work. It was such a good feeling to know that my pastors, friends, and family would be praying for Wayne and me.

Keithe and I went to the cafeteria and had breakfast. We kept reminding each other of the goodness of the Lord, and how He promised to never leave us or forsake us (Deuteronomy 31:6b, NIV). We then went to the waiting area where we sat down and covered up with blankets. It is always so cold in the hospital, and I'm a person who gets cold easily, so I was prepared with a couple of blankets, water, my Bible, and a few snacks for Keithe and me. We started talking about our childhood, and some of the funny things we did. We started laughing, and we'd remember another story, and we'd laugh more. This went on most of the day. We did go eat lunch in the cafeteria, but we continued to laugh. The nurse in surgery was great to call and inform us exactly what the surgeon was doing. We would begin to pray with our understanding and pray in the Spirit.

Later in the afternoon our son, Jonathan, came to the hospital to sit and wait with us. He would remember a story from his childhood, and we would all start laughing. Hour after hour we laughed until tears just rolled down our faces. Our oldest daughter, Heather, came around 4:00 p.m. and found us all cackling in laughter. I honestly believe this was a gift God gave us so we wouldn't be in worry and fretfulness. We were out of control with laughter. "A cheerful heart is good medicine…" (Proverbs 17:22, NLT). "The joy of the Lord is your strength" (Nehemiah 8:10, NLT).

At around 5:30 p.m., the nurse called and said that Wayne was being taken to recovery, and she would let us know when he was alert enough for us to go back and see him. She stated the surgery went well. Shortly afterward the surgeon came out to see us. He said Wayne did well, and that he was able to get the majority of the tumor on the brain stem except for a very small amount due to the doctor not wanting to penetrate the brain stem. He was able to remove all of the encapsulated tumor. He was not concerned about the small amount left. He said they'd have to wait until Wayne was alert enough to check if he was able to move his arms, and legs. This was the longest hour of waiting we had experienced, so we began to praise the Lord for His goodness and His mercy on Wayne and on us. I was so grateful to God for His presence being with us all day. Finally, the nurse came out to get us to go back to the recovery room. When we walked in, I told Keithe, "That's not Wayne." Since she was a nurse, she told me that Wayne's face and eyes were extremely swollen due to him lying face down for over 10 hours. She explained he would look better tomorrow. I had to be sure it was Wayne, so I looked at his hospital bracelet. It was shocking to see how very swollen his face was.

Suddenly, Wayne opened his eyes though they looked like slits. I asked him how he was feeling, and he began to cry with strong sobs as he raised his hands and arms, and said, "Praise God, Hallelujah!" We all started to thank God for His mercies toward Wayne. Then he put his hands out to me, Jonathan, and Heather to hold. He began singing to me, "You Are So Beautiful to Me" by Joe Cocker. Tears just poured down all our faces, with sobs of gratefulness to our Almighty God. God's very presence and Glory surrounded us all. I asked Wayne to move his toes and feet, and he did! What the devil meant for bad, God turned for good! "But thou, O Lord, art a shield for me; my glory and the lifter up of mine head" (Psalms 3:3, KJV).

For days Wayne stayed in the hospital while the swelling of his face and even his tongue gradually started to go back to normal. When we got home the surgeon had ordered Wayne to sleep in a reclining chair. Keithe was there and helped me get Wayne to the bathroom and helped with the bandages on the back of his neck. I was so incredibly grateful for her help, and just the companionship and support of my dear sister meant the world to me.

Two weeks later Wayne had his post-op appointment. The surgeon was incredibly pleased with his recovery and released him to do light activity, and even released him to go back to work since he had a desk job. Wayne continued to go back for MRIs every few years to make sure no tumors returned, but now he no longer has to do that.

Some miracles happen suddenly, and others happen gradually. I believe we'll be seeing more sudden miracles done by God through the laying on of hands in the years to come. God has given us doctors and surgeons also to assist in His care for our bodies, and I am so grateful to Him. "Let everything that hath breath **PRAISE THE LORD**" (Psalms 150:6, KJV). "Do you not know that your bodies are temples of the Holy Spirit, who is in you, whom you have received from God? You are not your own; you were bought at a price. Therefore, honor God with your bodies" (1 Corinthians 6:19-20, NIV).

11
Andrea's Prodigal Journey

After Andrea moved away from home at 19 years old, she involved herself with some people that would approach her with drugs. She would try the drugs but wasn't seeking to stay on drugs. We had no idea she was using drugs. People at work would approach her to try their drug of choice. Andrea became involved with a young man who also was using drugs off and on. He turned out to be very abusive. She was attending college, and they drove together to school. When the abuse became unbearable Andrea moved out. She dropped out of college because she didn't want to be in the same classes as this man.

Andrea continued working as a waitress. She was always a diligent worker at any job she had. One afternoon when she was working a tall, good looking man came in with several of his friends, and Andrea was their waitress. He was clean-cut and flirted with Andrea. He asked her if they could exchange phone numbers, which they did. For several days, they would talk on the phone and text each other, until he asked her out on a date. They seemed to really enjoy each other. Andrea was living with her sister, Jennifer, and she called us and said, "You're really going to like this guy. He's clean-cut, and wears Polo brand shirts." We laughed because we knew the brand of clothing you wear doesn't tell what type of person you are.

We finally met this man on my husband's birthday. Several of the family had gathered at the Olive Garden for dinner, and Andrea brought her boyfriend. He was 6'5" tall, attractive, and clean cut just like Jennifer said. He didn't talk much but he was able to carry on a conversation well. We were fairly impressed compared to the other men Andrea had dated.

Five weeks later, Andrea's boyfriend called Wayne to ask if he could marry Andrea and have our blessing. We were shocked since they barely knew each other, and we didn't know him. However, after a lengthy conversation, Wayne said yes, he could marry Andrea. Andrea and I went shopping for a wedding dress. It was fun watching her try on dress after dress, and talking about who she wanted in her wedding. I was looking for a carefree stylish Mother-of-the-Bride dress. It was such a good day shopping and planning for Andrea's wedding.

Two weeks later our church had a picnic, and Andrea and her fiancé asked if they could come and meet with us. Of course, we said yes. Andrea started telling us more about her fiancé. He barely said a word to us. She told us that he had been in prison for 3 years for drugs, and had only recently gotten out, which was when she met him. Our breathing became tight at this news. We always told our children to say no to drugs and no to those who had taken drugs due to the influence it could be on their lives. But here we were. Andrea also told us that he had a 5-year-old daughter. We already knew the difficulties of that in our family. However, the last thing she told us was a big bomb shell! She told us that they were already married! We were shocked and very disappointed.

There wasn't anything we could do about this situation. Andrea was a 25-year-old adult, and her husband was 27 years old. A week later we were invited to have lunch with her mother-in-law and her boyfriend. His mom was nice, but appeared irritated by the marriage situation. Andrea and her husband appeared to be quite satisfied. At this point, they had moved in with his mom until they were able to get a rent house.

They found and fixed up a rent house and had decent furniture. On several Sundays we went over and had pizza with them after church. We were introduced to his daughter on one of those Sundays. She was a sweet, intelligent child. We found out that Andrea's mother-in-law was very protective and partial to this granddaughter over everyone in her family. Andrea had to walk very carefully concerning her stepdaughter.

Everything seemed to be going well for them until January of 2009. Andrea was complaining of feeling nauseated and weak for days on end. She finally went to the doctor and found out she was 2½ months pregnant. What should've been a very exciting time turned out to be a nightmare.

Andrea's husband was furious and started rejecting her. He didn't want any more responsibilities. He would be gone on weekends and tell her he was camping with friends. His mom said that couldn't be possible because he had never been camping before. He wouldn't answer his phone when he was out, and he wouldn't answer his phone or texts when he was at work. Andrea was desperate to have her husband back. Instead, Andrea found out that her husband was back on drugs. Both of them had been introduced to Meth by his mom while living at her house, but Andrea said she didn't continue on it, yet Jared did. It was an exceedingly long and emotional nine months of pregnancy for her. Where was God in all of this?

The night Andrea went into labor, she had to beg him to come home and take her to the hospital. She called Wayne and me to please come to the hospital, and she called her mother-in-law, also. Her husband drove her to the hospital and dropped her off by herself. He was high on dope and didn't want to be there. Andrea was almost hysterical going through labor without her husband. Once she finally gave birth, Andrea wept, she said she had never wanted to be a single parent, but here she was.

The next day Andrea's husband came to the hospital for one hour. He held his new daughter, and barely said anything while he was there. I was there and could feel the pain Andrea was going through. When Andrea was discharged, we were with her. We took her to her house, but the lock was changed. Andrea's husband was there with his latest girlfriend. We had to call the police just to get the baby's and Andrea's clothes. Andrea then went to stay with her sister, Jennifer and her family. Andrea was deeply depressed for several months. All we could do was pray and ask God to intervene in all this craziness.

Time passed, and Andrea went to stay at her mother-in-law's house. She saw her husband off and on, and started back on Meth. After a couple of months, her mother-in-law called us and told us to come and get Andrea and the baby because Andrea was knocked out on drugs.

We drove to Tulsa to get them, and when we picked them up, I was extremely angry with the mother-in-law and Andrea's husband for introducing Andrea to Meth, and for his lack of responsibility in caring for them. They stayed with us in Muskogee for a couple of months until Andrea was able to find an apartment in Tulsa.

Once Andrea moved, she really appeared to be doing well. Her husband was in and out of jail so

Andrea only saw him periodically. Then there was the night where two guys broke into her apartment and held Andrea and her daughter at gunpoint. They ransacked the house and stole multiple items they could sell for cash. These guys were after her husband for what he owed them. Andrea was terrified!

We then found out that Andrea was back on Meth, and her husband was arrested again for dealing Meth. This time he went back to prison, and Andrea found out she was pregnant again. She moved into a rent house, and got off of Meth. This birth was more peaceful, with her mother-in-law and me at her side, and Wayne in the waiting room. This second child was as peaceful, and beautiful as the first baby girl.

After several months, Andrea was back on Meth. Now she was wrapping Meth and smuggling it to her husband when she went for prison visits. She was making $3,000 on these visits, which she used for more Meth. This went on for about three years. Andrea continued to sell to others as well. Unfortunately, she had become a part of a drug ring. We hadn't known she was back on drugs or selling it.

I was in training to become a Court Appointed Special Advocate (CASA) for foster children. As they talked to us about drugs and the symptoms of Meth use and other drugs, I had a revelation that Andrea was back on Meth again. It had been several years since we first saw her on drugs, and we had not noticed any symptoms until this training session pointed out more distinct behaviors. I felt devastated. I talked to Wayne, and we were talking with our other children about a family intervention to get her into a drug rehabilitation center.

Then one morning after Andrea took the girls to school, the Police busted Andrea in her home. They found three guns, Meth, and stacks of cash. They had been watching Andrea for at least a year. Andrea asked one officer if he would please call her sister, Heather, and have her pick up the girls at school, and give her the key to the house so she could get the girls' clothes. She requested the officer not to call the Department of Human Services (DHS). He agreed, and Andrea was taken to jail.

Heather picked up the girls' clothes, and toys, and took them to her apartment which she shared with a friend. She then picked up the girls at school and brought them to her apartment. They just didn't understand where their mommy was or why they couldn't see her. It was a difficult time for them all. Andrea was bailed out by her new lawyer and found a house in Broken Arrow, Oklahoma just outside of Tulsa. We obtained a lawyer for us to get guardianship with Heather of the girls. It was difficult convincing Andrea that this was best for the girls' sake so that DHS would not step in and take custody. Finally, Andrea signed the legal papers giving the three of us guardianship.

For the next two years, we were harassed weekly by her lawyer trying to get back custody of the girls and accusing us of various things. Our finances and emotions were drained in this fight to protect our two granddaughters. BUT GOD had another plan! "So be strong and courageous! Do not be afraid and do not panic before them. For the Lord your God will personally go ahead of you. He will neither fail you nor abandon you" (Deuteronomy 31:6, NLT).

During my prayer time one day I felt impressed to pray for the Lord to do whatever it took to get this lawyer out of our lives and out of Andrea's life. Two weeks later we were notified by our lawyer that Andrea's lawyer was visiting a client in jail and handed him her cell phone. This is against the law! The jail guard saw it and he and the lawyer wrestled for the phone. The guard was able to take custody of the phone and report it. This lawyer was put on suspension, and a month later she was disbarred! We found out that she was the lawyer for all the drug ring, and she was also busted for using and dealing drugs. The next time we went to court over the guardianship one of the other lawyers was there to apologize for what his partner had put us through, and he agreed with the guardianship and set visitations. All we could say was "Look what the Lord has done!"

Later the girls, and Heather moved down to Muskogee to live with us. They were there for two and a half years. It was a challenging time, but we tried to bring some kind of order into their lives. The girls were traumatized from not being with their mom. We enrolled them into counseling for a while, but we only saw slight changes in their attitudes. They were angry, traumatized, and unwilling to talk in counseling, especially the oldest girl.

When Andrea went back into court regarding her case, she was immediately taken by the Feds, and now her case was a Federal case. She was so scared! They put her in jail until they could schedule a Federal hearing. She would call me and cry and ask me to get her out, but we couldn't. She had chosen this life, and she would have to pay the price. We had people praying for her and we asked God to please make a way for her to go to a rehab. She was given a very experienced Federal lawyer who let her know she could choose jail or rehab. Our prayers were answered, she chose rehab.

For the next six months Andrea lived by the rules of the rehab. She took several classes learning to live drug free. Getting clean was painful, but we were surprised how well she did. She was mostly a model patient. We would take the girls to visit her every Sunday after church. They loved their time with Andrea, and Andrea loved being with her girls. We were immensely proud of Andrea.

Six months was over, and Andrea had another court appearance to determine if she was being sentenced to a Federal prison in another state or to be released on probation. We asked our pastor, who knew Andrea and what she'd been through, to write a letter to the judge. We wrote a letter of support, and Andrea's siblings wrote letters in support of her. The day of the hearing our family gathered with her lawyer, and we prayed for God's favor to be in the heart of the judge.

"For His anger is but for a moment, and His favor is for a lifetime! Weeping may tarry for the night, but joy comes with the morning"
Psalms 30:5, NLT

Just before entering the court room, Andrea broke down in deep weeping. We all held her and encouraged her to believe that God was with her. Our family filled one long bench in the court room. Andrea was called to the judge's bench. She looked so small standing there in this exceptionally large room. All I could do was pray and praise God quietly. The judge read the charges, and then she talked about Andrea's rehab report, and the many letters that were sent to her on Andrea's behalf. She remarked about our family all being there with Andrea and said all of this made her believe that it would not do any good for Andrea to go to a federal prison. She felt our family along with Andrea's determination to stay clean and get her children back, was a very strong force for Andrea's total recovery.

She pronounced Andrea to be on probation for five years, and weekly reports to her probation officer and submit to routine urine screens. God's favor, and abundant grace had set Andrea free! Now it was time for Andrea to prove she could stay free with the help, and strength of God. "Jesus replied, 'I tell you the truth, everyone who sins is a slave of sin. A slave is not a permanent member of the family, but a son is part of the family forever. So If the Son sets you free, you are truly free'" (James 8:34-36, NLT).

Andrea got her children back and was doing well. Her husband got out of prison and stayed with them for a year. Then one day he left with Andrea's best friend. This trauma affected all of them. Andrea had a short setback, but we were there to take care of the girls while Andrea recovered. She has been drug free for 8 years now, Praise God!

Andrea was such a help to my family when my twin sister passed away two year ago. She and her boyfriend totally remodeled my sister's house so we could get it ready to sell. She and her boyfriend are doing well. The girls are attending church and youth group regularly.

The girls continue to struggle in school. Public schools have so many traumatized children from being in Foster Care to being in homes with drug abusers, to verbal and physical abuse and neglect. Teachers and administrators think these kids are just "bad kids" or "rebellious." Most are kids living in trauma. How are they to concentrate on learning when there is abuse or neglect happening to them at home, or deep grief from being put in Foster Care? I don't have all the answers, but I know there are programs out there that will help these special children to learn.

My prayer is for God to bring Andrea, and her girls to the place where they can receive break-throughs from the trauma. I pray for them to receive deliverance, and healing from the past so they can be productive citizens, and witnesses of God's mercy and grace. I know God is faithful and trustworthy! He has a plan and purpose for each of them, and inner healing is God's specialty! "Behold, I am doing a new thing; now it springs forth, do you not perceive it? I will make a way in the wilderness, and rivers in the desert" (Isaiah 43:19, ESV). "For I know the plans I have for you, says the Lord, They are plans for good and not for evil, to give you a future and a hope" (Jeremiah 29:11, TLB).

12
The End of Her Journey

After Keithe recovered fully from breast cancer in 1991, she returned to nursing and retired in 2010. She had a full career and worked in the hospital in surgery, pediatrics, newborns, and ER. She also worked for doctors in private practice, and in Home Health Care. She mostly loved Home Health Care because she was able to spend more time getting to know and serving individual people and their families. Keithe was very gregarious. She never met a stranger and made many friends.

After retiring she spent more time with her husband, Gene, and her grandchildren. She loved to shop! She usually found something to her liking at Dillard's, and Brighton's. She loved bright colors. Her husband gave her elegant jewelry on special occasions like her birthday, and Christmas.

Her hair was a brassy red color which she had styled 2 times a week. She also loved going to the manicurist to have her nails painted with beautiful art designs once every three weeks. Keithe was a very classy lady.

Keithe also had a very loud infectious laugh. Sometimes her friends were embarrassed by her loud laugh, but then they'd start laughing hard too. She was a joy! She and her friends, loved to go out to eat, and go to the movies. If it was a funny movie Keithe would be cackling raucously, and others would start laughing because of her laughter. If it was a sad movie she would be sobbing with the characters. When I visited Keithe I loved going to the movies with her. She was so much fun to be with.

I loved going to visit Keithe in Florida. She and I went on a Caribbean cruise once and had so much fun. We were dressed in our formals for dinner one night, and as we walked into the dining room Keithe caught her heel on the rug. She immediately fell flat on her face! I was stunned! Everyone Oooohed! Men jumped up to help her up. She started laughing and said, "How's that for a grand entrance!" Everyone laughed with her. Thank God she wasn't hurt physically. I'm sure her ego was a little hurt; whose wouldn't be! That's the kind of humor Keithe had.

After my dad passed away my mom and I went to Florida for several years in May to just sit in the sun and walk on the beach. Keithe would get off work and drive an hour to have dinner with us, and on Saturday we would shop a bit. These have been great memories for me.

In 2015, Keithe was diagnosed with Idiopathic Pulmonary Fibrosis (IPF). It is a rare, progressive illness of the respiratory system, characterized by the thickening and stiffening of lung tissue. Its symptoms include gradual shortness of breath, and a dry uncontrollable cough. When she was diagnosed the doctors couldn't tell her how long she had to live because it was such an unpredictable disease. However, most people with IPF live between two and five years.

She was determined to spend more time with her husband, daughters Chrissy, and Terri, and her grandchildren. Terri lived an hour and 15 minutes away from her mom. She had six children and every time there was a family birthday, Christmas, Thanksgiving, etc. Keithe would drive to their home and spend hours laughing and enjoying her family's love. Terri spoke with her mom daily, and her children called their Keke often to share their experiences, and for advice as they were growing up.

Keithe's oldest daughter, Chrissy, lived in Colorado at the time. Several times a week, she would call her mom, and they would have their mother-daughter talks with many laughs and some tears. Chrissy's two sons were in the Army and went to visit Keithe as often as they were able. Chrissy and her youngest son tried to go more often. Keithe asked me every year for five years to visit her at Thanksgiving. It was a joy for me to go even though I had to leave my family and ask them to sacrifice this holiday. I knew it would only be temporary, and I didn't know how long she had to live.

When **IPF** progressed Keithe had to use an oxygen machine at home and carry a portable oxygen machine when leaving the house. The cough increased. It would drain her of her energy. She got to the point where she had to put the portable oxygen tank in a pull bag with wheels. She just didn't have the strength to carry the bag anymore. She continued to go to her hairdresser, and her manicurist because it brought some peace and joy for her.

Keithe's daughter, Chrissy, was struggling with why God had brought her and her family to Colorado. BUT GOD had a plan to use Chrissy. "You didn't choose Me, but I chose you and appointed you to go and produce lasting fruit, so that the Father will give you whatever you ask for, using My name"(John 15:16, NLT) Chrissy's sister, Terri, had been researching what could help their mom not to have so much pain. She finally found a product made in Colorado that was helping people with pain. It was specifically "Charlotte's Web CBD oil." It was expensive but the family agreed to have Keithe try it. Since Chrissy lived in Colorado, she was able to buy it and then ship it to Keithe in Florida. Chrissy suddenly realized that was why God had her in Colorado. Keithe tried it, and it helped with the pain! She used it for over 7 months.

My last visit with Keithe was Thanksgiving 2019. Keithe called several times to make sure I was coming. I confirmed that I was. She told me that Chrissy was coming to visit on her birthday, December 18th. When I arrived, I knew things were worse. Even though we had been talking on the phone a couple times a week, it was different to see Keithe, and see how she mobilized. She was very tired. I noticed her unrelenting cough had stopped. I had to help her by pulling the oxygen tank for her when we went out, or I had to go into the grocery store for her. She had become a little curt, and she also fell asleep several times a day due to the exhaustion of just trying to breathe.

On Thanksgiving, she and I drove to Terri's mother-in-law's house for their family Thanksgiving. Keithe would not let me drive. She insisted on driving. The grandkids, Terri, and I helped get Keithe whatever she needed. They had things set up cafeteria-style for dinner. Keithe had her portable oxygen tank, so we all helped get her food for her. It seemed like she wasn't getting quite enough oxygen from the portable tank. She was quite tired.

After dinner, everyone helped to clean up. Then Terri's family, Keithe, and I went outside to take pictures. You couldn't tell by the picture how weak she was, but we knew. When we got back to Keithe's house, she gave a plate of food to her husband who didn't go with us. She was so tired. She fell asleep that night early in her recliner.

The next day Keithe had her nail appointment. I pulled her portable oxygen in a wheeled bag as she walked ahead of me. A lady there asked Keithe if we were mother and daughter. This upset her, but I told her I had better make-up than she did that covered my wrinkles better. We laughed. Keithe always had such beautiful nails with nail art, and she always had her hair colored a bright reddish/auburn color.

One afternoon we began to go through the clothes in her closet; she had a big walk-in closet that was full of her impeccable clothes. She had lost so much weight that she had to buy other clothes in smaller sizes. I would pull out an article and she'd decide to give it away or not. We worked for over an hour with her sitting in a chair and me folding discarded clothes. This was difficult knowing that she would not be living much longer.

Two days later it was time for me to leave. Again, she wouldn't let me drive, and she didn't ask her husband, Gene, to take me to the airport. We talked a lot about family and things on the way. It had been a good visit. When we got to the airport in Tampa, we looked at each other with tears in our eyes and we told each other how very much we loved each other as sisters and best friends. We both knew it would be the last time we would ever see each other. I got my luggage out of the car, threw her a kiss, and said I love you one last time. It was a somber flight home. I prayed that God would not let her suffer long and that he would comfort and strengthen Gene, Chrissy, Terri, and the grandkids through the process. BUT GOD had a special plan.

For the next seven months, we called each other three times a week. Some things that we talked about she didn't remember any more. We talked about her wanting her good jewelry to go to her two daughters, and granddaughters. She wanted some of her other jewelry to go to the three of us sisters.

By the first of July of 2020, Keithe had trouble talking on the phone. Her daughter Chrissy had been flying back and forth from Tennessee, where she had moved, to help her mom for the past three to four months. Chrissy placed a Facetime call to me so I could see and hear my sister. Keithe was weak. She told me she was tired of fighting, and she was ready to go be with the Lord. I told her that I was releasing her to the Lord, and how very much I loved her. I told her to give my love to Mama and Daddy, and I'd see her when God says it's my turn. I told Chrissy that each of their family members needed to tell Keithe they were releasing her to the Lord. Some people psychologically can't allow themselves to pass because their family can't let them go.

By July 16th, Hospice had been there daily, and meds were administered that kept Keithe sedated, and free from anxiety and pain. Chrissy, Terri, and Gene were by her bed. Chrissy was videotaping when suddenly Keithe opened her eyes wide, looked up, then at them, and said in a strong voice "My goodness, praise God!" Her daughter Terri said, "Are you seeing something Mama?" Then she said, "Aren't we so happy! Aren't we happy! Oh my gosh, this is wonderful! This is wonderful! Oh my God! We're gonna see God together! Do you know that? Oh my God!" She was awake for a short while, and then she closed her eyes and didn't awaken again. "These things I have spoken to you, that My joy may be in you, and that your joy may be full" (John 15:11, ESV). What an amazing act by God to help the family know that Keithe was already sensing God and what joy she was feeling! I was so thankful that Chrissy videoed these last special moments with my precious sister.

The next day, July 17, Keithe passed on to be with the Lord. "Therefore you now have sorrow; but I will see you again and your heart will rejoice, and your joy no one will take from you"(John 16:22, NKJV). It was a time of sorrow, but it was laced with such joy knowing she had no more pain, and she was with her Savior, and God. What a legacy of faith and dependency on God Keithe's life had been. She had been a born-again, Spirit-filled, Christian for 50 years, and had weathered so many heart-wrenching storms in her life that only God could have helped her through.

Keithe was a very classy lady inwardly, and outwardly. She had a loud-spirited laugh, and a Howdy Doody smile that commanded a room. She dearly loved her family, and always told them so. Perfect, she was not, but she tenaciously followed her Lord and Savior Jesus Christ.

An interesting thing about Keithe's birthday and date of passing is that she was born on February 7th, and passed on July 17th. July is the 7th month. In the Bible, the number 7 means completion. From birth on the 7th to passing on 7-17 she had completed her race and journey. Praise God!

13
Me and My Shadow

On January 13, 1948, Kitty and I were born in Muskogee, Oklahoma. We were identical twins that were born on twin nurses' birthday. It was noteworthy enough that our local paper had a picture of us in the nurses' arms. So, we said we were celebrities from the time we were born.

We had an older sister, Keithe, who was three years older than we were, and later we had another sister, Candy, who was three years younger. When we were seven years old, we moved to Lapel, Indiana with Brockway Glass Co. We were known in Lapel as the four Carlton girls. Most people couldn't tell the difference between Kitty and me, so they just called us "the twins." It was difficult to have our own identities being twins. We dressed alike until

Junior High School. We had the same friends until we were juniors in High School. We were both in the band. She played the clarinet, and I played the trumpet and French horn.

We were both in the school chorus, she sang soprano, and I sang alto. During the town's fish fry, they had a talent show and Kitty and I sang "Me and My Shadow." In Junior High we were cheerleaders together. In High School we were B Team cheerleaders until our senior year when I was voted cheerleader, but she wasn't. This caused a lot of strain on our relationship. Yet Kitty was determined to be something special, so she started the Strutting Corp with six members. They carried flags and did routines with the marching band.

We both made good grades until we had to take Algebra and Geometry. Kitty did great with math, but I never could comprehend it. Despite tutoring I just couldn't get it. I got Ds in both classes. One time we decided to dress alike for school, and Kitty went to my classes, and I went to her classes. It was all fun until it was time to go to her Geometry class. The teacher decided to do a pop quiz. I was so freaked out. I took the test and failed it.

At the end of the day, we told her math teacher about us switching classes as a joke, and we asked if he would allow Kitty to take the test. He said NO! He said this was the price we had to pay. Kitty never forgave me for this. Even in adult life she would tell our kids and other people about me failing her math test.

One night we were double dating, and we decided to switch dates. It was a fun night. Later we told the guys that we had switched on them. The problem after the date was that Kitty's date started liking me, and he broke up with her. I did not date him! That wouldn't have been fair to Kitty.

When we graduated from High School, Daddy was promoted and transferred back to Muskogee, Okla. Kitty decided to go to business school in Indianapolis, so she moved back to Lapel. I had decided to go to an all girls junior college, Gulf Park Women's College in Gulf Port, Mississippi. Kitty was doing well because she was living with friends. I, on the other hand, was so very homesick. I had never made friends on my own before, and it was so painful. I yearned to be home with my parents, and with Kitty. I spent a lot of time eating ice cream, and sleeping in when I should have been in class. At the end of the first semester, I had a grade average of 1.5. After Christmas vacation I was better adjusted. I was able to spend time with Kitty, my parents, and Candy. My grade average came up, and I came back the next year and achieved a 3.8 grade average and was on the President's Honor Roll.

A few years later, Kitty and I both got married and later we both had a baby six months apart. Our next 2 children were also six months apart. I can assure you that it was not planned that way. Wayne and I went on and had 2 more children. Kitty had 1 girl and 2 boys, and we had 4 girls and then a boy. Kitty and I had always been close, but we were also competitive. Twins are like that. Some are extremely close and need to do everything together. They continue to dress alike, and are just incredibly involved with each other as adults. Other twins are close, but they are competitive.

I remember one time I had saved and saved to buy a pretty suit. When Kitty saw it, she went right down to the store and bought a suit just like it. I was so furious with her. We were attending the same church and there was no way we could ever wear the suit on the same Sunday.

We started a Christian singing group named "Sharing" that had Wayne as the bass player, a lead guitar player, a piano player, and a drummer. Wayne, Kitty, and I were the singers. At least we were able to wear our look-a-like suits when we went to different churches to sing. Kitty and her husband were able to take nice trips, and I would want to take a trip too, but we had five children, and the expenses were great. We also had our children in a Christian school. Later, Kitty and her family moved to Tulsa, Oklahoma where they put their kids in a Christian school.

Kitty and I tried to help each other in many family situations. The most painful situation was when her husband of twenty-seven years divorced her. The emotional pain she felt was unexplainable. It hit me so deep in my heart and soul that it almost felt like it was happening to me. I frequently went to Tulsa to stay with her. I held her in bed as she wept and wept. She was frightened for so many reasons. The love of her life had left her. He also had planned it and put his money in his dad's trust so he wouldn't have to pay her anything. She had to move out of her home, get an apartment, and find a job, which was traumatic since she hadn't worked in twenty-seven years. There was a river of tears from both of us. As years went by, Kitty struggled financially, and emotionally. I often went to Tulsa to support her. I would take her out to eat, and she would pour her heart out as I listened. Sometimes I was able to stay for three days at a time. She was so very lonely, and when she wasn't working, she would be in bed sleeping to escape.

In September of 2014, Kitty was living in Tulsa, but driving to Muskogee for her job as a bookkeeper for the Salvation Army. It was an hour drive. Kitty had never been a morning person. She frequently received reprimands for being late to her previous jobs. On this day, Kitty was driving on the turnpike toward Muskogee when suddenly she hit the concrete median. She was shocked, and dizzy. She then hit it another time.

She remembered thinking 'I have to get off the highway.' She said she swerved to the right lane and over into the grass and hit a raised embankment which made her car roll several times and end up upside down over a small water pond. She said she was so dizzy and tried to reach her glove compartment to get a special knife to cut the seat belt, but she couldn't reach it. She said she was praying and crying out to God for help. Suddenly she heard a man's voice. He said he had been following her on the highway when he saw her hit the median twice, and then go off the highway and roll. He told her not to worry, he had called 911.

When the Highway Patrol and ambulance arrived, they said it was a good thing this man saw her car roll because it was not visible from the highway. She told them she tried to get the knife, and they told her it was a good thing that she didn't get it because cutting the seat belt would've caused much more injuries to her neck and body.

We received a call from the Highway Patrol telling us Kitty had an accident, and she was being transported to St. John's Hospital in Tulsa. I called Wayne, and we drove to Tulsa to the hospital. We prayed all the way there asking God to help Kitty, and to heal her of any injuries. She said she didn't know what happened or what caused her to hit the wall. Her ankle and foot were basically shattered, and she needed surgery. While family was around her bed talking to her, I noticed her eyes shifted and she quit talking for a few seconds. I called in the nurse and told her I thought Kitty was having seizures. She did this several times and even asked what happened when she would become alert again. Later the doctors did tests and found that she was having Petit Mal Seizures. She had never had these before. We never found out if these seizures had caused the accident or not, BUT GOD did protect her from death, and from more major injuries.

> *"Fear not, for I am with you; be not dismayed, for I am your God; I will strengthen you, yes, I will help you, I will uphold you with my righteous right hand"*
> *Isaiah 41:10, NKJV*

Kitty was in the hospital for two weeks. She wanted to go home, but she required care and physical therapy. She was placed in a skilled unit of a nursing home. She was so very frustrated because she had bills to pay, but of course, she could not work.

Two of my granddaughters were very close to Kitty. Ryleigh and Kamryn called her KiKi. We would drive up every Sunday after church to visit Kitty. We would wheel her outside in the wheelchair, and the girls would run and push "Kiki" all around the area until she would become tired. Kitty loved the girls' visits, and looked forward to them weekly. Kitty became friends with several of those in the nursing home and always talked about Jesus with them. She spent about six weeks in the facility, and finally was discharged and came home.

She was able to get Home Health Care, but she had to learn how to scoot around in a wheelchair and hop on one foot into the bathroom. We had to get her on Meals on Wheels so she could eat at noon. I would go to Tulsa once a week and buy easy prep food for her so she could eat dinner. It took quite a while, but she was finally able to walk slowly. She never did get full healing and use of her ankle, but she was grateful just to be able to walk at all. "And we know that all things work together for good to them that love God, to them who are the called according to His purpose" (Romans 8:28, KJV).

She also had to learn to live on her Social Security, which was desperately difficult. Several times Keithe, Candy, and I gave her extra money for bills, and food. There were three of our classmates from high school who knew of her plight, were praying for her, and sent her money. She felt so embarrassed but was very grateful for her dear friends and family who helped her.

Then in 2018 after having a Mammogram the doctor found a very small lump. Her doctor ordered a breast biopsy. Of course we were praying for good results. However, it came back positive for Cancer. Kitty was frightened because our mom, and our oldest sister, Keithe, both had cancer. Mom's cancer was so minimal that they removed the breast, and she had no other treatment.

Keithe's cancer was stage 4, and she survived the treatments. Kitty's doctor said they would remove the breast tissue and do radiation at that time. Her cancer was between the first an second stage. BUT GOD was watching over Kitty again, and His praises, and His Word were in her mouth daily. "Let the high praises of God be in their mouth, and a two-edge sword in their hand"(Psalm 149:6, NLT).

Our family and many friends prayed for Kitty to recover completely with no further treatment. Kitty had a three-hour surgery, and the doctors even did radiation in that area where the breast tissue had been to make sure all cancer cells were killed. The doctors stated it all went very well. They didn't think she'd need any other treatment, but she was scheduled for frequent checkups with five different doctors.

Kitty was determined to be a blessing and a witness of Jesus Christ every time she had to go to the Cancer Treatment Center of Tulsa. Their bus would take her to the Center, and I would drive up and meet her there. She was a beam of light and joy from the moment she checked in until she checked out, which sometimes was three hours later. She would greet people and ask to pray for them, or tell them Jesus loved them, or just listen to them talk and tell their story. Sometimes we would also be silly by trying on hats in the shop, and having others take our pictures. Other times they would have a musician and singer singing Christian songs and we would participate with hands raised as we worshiped our God and Savior. Kitty never required any other treatment, and she was so grateful.

Kitty continued having difficulty walking, and she had issues with Osteoporosis in her back that required several outpatient procedures. Some worked and some didn't. The main thing was that she would have to use a walker for the rest of her life unless God did a miracle. She continued her praise and worship to God for just being alive. She knew God was her only hope.

In March of 2021, Kitty was home by herself when she started having some chest pains and pressure. It concerned her but she prayed and asked the Lord to remove the pain and pressure. That did not happen, and it even got worse. She didn't want to be fearful, so she continued to pray and declare the healing Word of God. She started breaking out in a sweat and realized it was time to call 911. BUT GOD was with her. "Then call on Me when you are in trouble, and I will rescue you, and you will give Me glory" (Psalm 50:15, NLT).

At the hospital they determined Kitty had had a mild heart attack. They found a blockage and were able to go in and place a stint in the artery. She had no difficulties and was able to come home in three days. She also had no remedial problems. Kitty and all of us were so incredibly grateful to God for protecting her, and we gave Him all the glory. Kitty had had so many adverse things happen to her in her lifetime, but she always praised God during her troubles. That doesn't mean she never questioned God, because she did, but she knew God was her source of strength to endure whatever happened.

In the summer of 2021, Kitty started having a cough. She said she would get this tickle in her throat and needed to cough. A month later the cough was getting stronger and more persistent. The doctor did an x-ray of the lungs and there didn't appear to be anything concerning. So, he gave her some cough medicine.

By the fall of 2021, Kitty was coughing profusely. It bothered her, but what concerned her the most was not knowing why she was coughing so often and so hard. Sometimes she would be talking and suddenly start coughing. It progressively got worse to the point that she finally had to have oxygen at home. She mostly slept on her couch with her head propped up. She stopped going out unless it was for a very important doctor's visit. Many times, her best friend Judy Burns would take her to her doctor's appointments, and sometimes when I was able to take time off from work, I would take her. Kitty was growing increasingly concerned about her health. It was such a task for her to just get dressed to go to the doctor. Several times she would get up, get dressed, and then call the doctor and cancel her appointment because she was so very exhausted from getting dressed, and just could not go.

On Christmas of 2021, Stephen, her youngest son, had our whole family and Kitty over for Christmas dinner. Kitty had dressed so nicely like she used to do. She even had make-up on her face. We had our picture taken together, and it showed how much shorter she had gotten from Osteoporosis. It broke my heart to see her like this. We all ate dinner, and then Kitty laid down on the couch. She was so exhausted from just being up. Just when she'd fall asleep, she'd start coughing.

January, February, and March of 2022 saw Kitty's cough becoming stronger and stronger. She said she felt like she was strangling from the cough. Finally in April her doctor did more in-depth testing and diagnosed Kitty with Idiopathic Pulmonary Fibrosis. It is a serious disease that causes irreversible scarring of the lungs. It progresses over time. The scarring makes it hard to breathe, and eventually the lungs can't inhale oxygen. There is no known cause or cure, and the doctors say it is not hereditary.

I've formed my own opinion after losing my oldest sister, Keithe, and now Kitty was also diagnosed with Idiopathic Pulmonary Fibrosis. Both Keithe, and Kitty had radiation for cancer. My theory is that the radiation caused the onset of IPF. It's the only common denominator between Keithe and Kitty besides their genes.

I spent several weekends with Kitty after the diagnosis, yet I thought she had several more years to live. We had to start turning the oxygen up to eight so she could get enough oxygen to breathe. She decided she wanted Hospice to start coming in along with Home Health Care in which she'd been receiving services. She knew she needed all these services even though it made her realize her own mortality.

In June of 2022, Kitty's doctor told her she was dying. She told her three adult children what the doctor said. Kitty had prayed diligently for the last several years that her relationship with her daughter Michelle and son Michael would be healed. She had prayed that she would not die until her son Stephen found a Godly woman to marry, and that she would get to see them have a child. She also prayed she would not be alone when she died. I just could not believe that she was dying! She looked fairly healthy even though she was on oxygen.

It just did not register with me. "The steadfast love of the Lord never ceases; His mercies never come to an end; they are new every morning; great is your faithfulness" (Lamentations 3:22-23, ESV).

BUT GOD, who is the author and finisher of our faith heard Kitty's heart felt prayers and saw her faith and trust in Him.

When she told Michael and Michelle that she was dying they both started coming over to see her regularly. They each asked Kitty for her forgiveness, and she asked them for their forgiveness. Relationships were being mended, and Kitty was feeling so much more peaceful.

Her son, Stephen, had renewed a relationship with a friend he had in high school who was a strong Christian. Tiffany lived in Louisiana, but that didn't interrupt their relationship. Tiffany started driving to Tulsa to see Stephen, and she even helped Kitty when she was here. This relationship was serious.

Also in June, Stephen received a phone call from a lady he had had a couple of dates with four years previous. She told him that she had a 4-year-old son that she believed to be his. She had been with another man who had told her not to tell Stephen about the baby. But now she felt like she needed to tell him her suspicions. Stephen was shocked, and he insisted on a paternity test. The test came back 99.9% positive that Stephen was the father. Stephen was able to meet his son and start learning about this little blessing that had come to him. He introduced Rhys to his grandmother, Kiki. Kitty cried and was so amazed at this friendly and loving little guy. She hugged him and he hugged her back. Her heart was so full. What a miracle!

In July, Stephen had to go to Qatar for business for three weeks. He was very nervous about going and leaving Kitty. So Heather, my oldest daughter, volunteered to stay with Kitty. Heather had her own health issues, and had not been able to work. However, she was able to prepare food, and walk with Kitty to the bathroom. Kitty used a walker so that helped. During these three weeks Kitty had several coughing attacks that scared her and literally took her breath away. Heather said it was frightening to watch and not be able to help her Aunt Kitty. Nighttime was the worst because Heather was a sound sleeper. Stephen had a camera installed that Tiffany could watch to see on her phone if Kitty's oxygen tubes were secure on her nose. Several times she would have to call Heather to put the cannula back in Kitty's nose. They even had to tape it on her face.

When Stephen came home from his trip, he knew Kitty was no longer able to stay in her home by herself, and even if he came by every day, it was too dangerous for her to remain at home. While he was gone someone had tried to break into Kitty's house, and Kitty and Heather had been terrified. Plus, the danger of Kitty's health situation warranted a change. Stephen made a very difficult decision and told Kitty she needed to come and stay with him. He was going to take a leave of absence from his work for however long it would be. Kitty did not want to leave her own home.

Stephen continued to tell her why she could not stay, and what he would do for her. Kitty told Stephen she would give him two weeks, and if she didn't feel comfortable, she wanted to come back to her house. Stephen agreed.

On August 1, 2022, Stephen moved Kitty into one of his guest bedrooms where there was a nice big window to look out. He had a hospital bed with a special mattress, a flat screen television, a reclining chair, and several family pictures in her room. He also brought her old Schnauzer, Ziggy. Ziggy was mostly blind, but he needed Kitty, and she needed him. Kitty was thrilled that Stephen would do this for her. She always feared dying alone. She was now having to wear a full oxygen mask at night. I still was not accepting that Kitty was dying.

Kitty had requested that her pastor, Sharon Daugherty of Victory Christian Center, come and pray for her. Kitty had been Pastor Sharon's assistant on Sunday mornings many years ago. Pastor Sharon came, and they had a very sweet time talking and praying together. Kitty had always loved Pastor Sharon's singing voice and had a couple of her CDs. Her son, Pastor Paul Daugherty, also came on another day. She loved his preaching and several of his songs. They reminisced, laughed, and talked about Jesus. Both of them prayed for God's peace for Kitty in the coming days.

Kitty and her best friend, Judy Burns, used to meet at Olive Garden and spend time talking about the Lord, and what was going on in America. One evening Judy brought food that Kitty liked from Olive Garden to Stephen's home. Stephen set up the atmosphere with Italian music, good china, and cloth napkins. Kitty loved every minute of it with her dear friend. They laughed and enjoyed each other's company. Judy had even said that Kitty didn't look like she was dying.

On August 28, 2022, Wayne and I went to Stephen's after church just like we had been doing all month and the months previously before she had moved. Kitty's granddaughter, Judy, whom Kitty called Lizzy, had come to visit from North Carolina, and to help with Kitty's care. Tiffany also was there and had been cooking as well as helping Stephen care for Kitty. Kitty and I sat on the side of the bed and talked about how good God had been to her. She stated the three things she had been praying about for the past several years. She talked about how through this illness God had brought her two oldest children back into a relationship with her, and how very much this meant to her. She said God was healing her heart and how amazing it felt. She stated how excited she was that Stephen and Tiffany were dating seriously, and how they both loved God and wanted to serve Him.

She spoke of the miracle God did in bringing Stephen's son, her grandson, to her, even though it was in a very unconventional way. She spoke of Stephen and how he had felt he needed to take care of her until she passed away. She was absolutely amazed at God, and what He had done for her! She continued to say that God had answered all her prayers, and even though He hadn't healed her body she was excited about going to be with Him. Then she said, "Can you believe this? Isn't this just awesome!" We both joyfully laughed at the goodness of God. We hugged each other, and I got teary eyed. She held my hand and said, "You're never going to be alone. Jesus and I will be with you." I just couldn't see that she was that close to dying. I thought it would be maybe in six months or so. She was able to sit up, and talk to me, and she still had her sense of humor. I just couldn't see it. We hugged and said, "I love you a bushel and a peck," which was our family's typical goodbye.

Stephen called me that week and told me that they were having to start Kitty on Lorazepam for anxiety and Morphine for pain. I was hesitant about her being on those two medications because I knew she wouldn't be awake much. She told me she wanted to be alert and awake as much as possible. But Hospice said due to the restlessness and pain it was time to start these medications.

Once they started the medications Kitty was never awake again. Occasionally she'd briefly open her eyes and say, "help me." When Kitty's daughter was in town, she, Stephen, Tiffany, and Heather took turns staying in the room with Kitty. Stephen, his sister, and Tiffany would alternate staying in her room at night, and Heather would mostly stay with her during the day. All of them were very attentive to Kitty's needs.

The next Sunday, September 4th, Wayne and I went to Stephen's after church as usual. I was stunned to see Kitty lying there with a full oxygen mask on her face, not moving, and not even aware that we were even there. Now it was becoming real to me. I didn't know how to prepare for this. Just last Sunday we were sitting on the side of her bed talking, and holding each other, and now a week later she was unresponsive.

On Monday I drove to Stephen's. Stephen, Heather, and I decided to go check out a couple of Hospice Homes. It was becoming extremely difficult for everyone to take care of all of Kitty's needs. School had started for me and I wasn't available like I wanted to be. We liked one Hospice Home specifically because they could roll her bed out on a balcony for her to get fresh air. We cried, but we agreed this would be best for everyone. Kitty would have 24-hour care, and we all would take turns sitting with her. We told the home we'd get all the information to them so Kitty could be admitted.

The next day Stephen called the Hospice home with all the information. When I drove up to Jenks, outside of Tulsa, Stephen told me the home had rejected our request because Kitty was in the last stage of dying. This didn't make any sense to me. I thought that was what the Hospice Home was for; to help those in the last stage of life. Now we were all just going to have to pull together to see Kitty through to the end.

On Wednesday several family members came to see Kitty. Stephen had arranged for a friend of his to come and spend a couple of hours playing the guitar and singing Christian songs to Kitty. Another friend came and played the piano and sang Christian songs to her. Our youngest sister, Candy, and her husband, Rick, drove up to be with Kitty. Our daughter Whitney drove up to Jenks just to sit and hold her Aunt Kitty's hand. Andrea and her girls, Ryleigh and Kamryn, came to sit with their "Kiki." Our son Jonathan had been coming over frequently to help support his cousin, Stephen. Our daughter Jennifer and her family came by off and on also. All of our family was pulling together to help as needed. Thursday, I drove back up to Stephen's home to take my turn in staying up all night with Kitty. He showed me the meds, and how to administer them

We talked about the med schedule that was written on a white board. He had Christian music playing softly in the room twenty-four-seven. He also had a camera in the room so he could see on his phone if his mom needed anything or was stirring. Heather was sitting in the room with Kitty while Stephen, Tiffany and I sat down in the kitchen and talked about the Hospice nurses and how good they were doing with Kitty.

After we ate, I went into the bedroom to sit with Kitty for the night. Stephen was not good at letting anyone else take care of his mom. Several times through the night he would come in and check about the medications, and how she was doing. Finally, at 3:00 a.m. I told him that I had come to relieve him from the night watch so he could get some sleep, but that wasn't happening. So, I told him he could either go get some sleep or he could come sit with his mom and I'd go get some sleep. He finally went to bed. His intentions were good, and he was being protective of his mom, but he was exhausted, and highly emotional.

It was a very long night. I didn't feel like I could just sit in the recliner and go to sleep. I felt like I needed to hold Kitty's hand. So, I moved the chair by her bed where I could hold her hand. I talked to Kitty and told her all the things I had forgotten to say to her. I reminisced about our childhood, and about how our kids had always been so close to each other as cousins. I talked to her about our sister Keithe, and Mama, and Daddy, who were all in Heaven. I read scriptures out loud to her, sang along with the music playing, and talked to God out loud. I asked the Lord to please not let Kitty suffer long, and to please take her quickly.

A couple times in the night Kitty would open her eyes, and try to sit up, and say "Help me!" Then she'd lay back down with her eyes closed. I'd answer her, "I'm trying to," and then I'd weep. I would pray in the Spirit, and with my understanding pleading with God to end this. I still praised and thanked God for who He was, and all He'd done for Kitty. By early morning I thought all was peaceful, but suddenly Kitty opened her eyes again, and tried to sit up, and said "kill me." I was so distraught! I wept and wept, and prayed louder, as if God couldn't hear me, for God to please take her.

The next day was Friday. Around 7:00 am Stephen came into the room. He asked how things were, and I told him we needed to go out into the big hallway. I told him about Kitty opening her eyes and trying to sit up and saying, "kill me." He was devastated. He began to cry and get angry with God for allowing her to suffer like this and questioning why. I had no answers for him.

During the day Hospice came over and checked on Kitty and her medications. They increased the dose of both meds so she would be more comfortable. There was a lot of family there all day. Several took turns sitting with Kitty.

Friday evening Kitty's son, Michael, and his wife, Mona, came over. They had just returned from a trip to Greece. Michael had called Kitty from Greece, and Stephen told him his mom wasn't able to respond, but he held the phone up to Kitty's ear, and Michael talked to his mom. It's a well-known fact that the hearing is the last sense to go, so we were glad Michael had called her. So, when Michael went into the room and saw his mom, he was shocked to see her unconscious, with a full oxygen mask on. This is not how she was last week before he left. He was confused why we didn't have her in the hospital. We had to explain that Kitty wanted Hospice, and to die at home at Stephen's. It was her choice. We explained that we had been taking turns staying up with her at night, and throughout the day. Michael was very upset because he didn't want her to suffer, and we explained about her medication, and how Hospice was helping us. He was really struggling with it all.

After Michael left, I went into Kitty's room to sit with her. I was praying scriptures out loud, and quietly singing along with the songs that were playing. It was about 10:00 pm when suddenly Kitty's breathing changed into a death rattle. The death rattle is a sound that is different in each patient who is dying. It signals that death is very near. On average, a person usually lives for around 25 hours after the death rattle begins and the last phase of the dying process begins. I didn't know that at the time. I heard this sound that sounded like my grandma when she passed away, and I suddenly became fully aware that my precious Kitty was really dying.

I became hysterical and ran out of the room and into the living room wailing with this revelation. The family took me outside on the patio and I continued to just wail and wail. It was so very deep, and I couldn't control it.

Stephen called Wayne to drive up, and they called Whitney to come up. All the rest of my family was there. I thought I was having a full breakdown. This wailing went on for over an hour. Then Wayne and Whitney arrived. Wayne tried to comfort me, but this revelation of my precious twin sister truly dying was so deeply painful for me. BUT GOD knowing what I needed gave me a vision of Kitty and me as babies with the umbilical cord connecting us. Then I heard Him say, "I'm cutting the umbilical cord so you can go on." What a loving Father that He would give me this revelation and understanding to hold on to. It would take time for me to fully comprehend what all this meant for me.

After a while I got up, and said I needed to go back to Kitty's room. The rattle had stopped. The whole family, including my 12-year-old granddaughter, Ryleigh, were in the room. Ten year old Kamryn was asleep on the couch.

There were eleven of us there. The music played and we all sang along. Everyone in our family is musically talented and the harmonies of our voices ushered in the very presence of God. We were worshiping the Lord amidst death. Then the song "**It is Well with My Soul**" began to play, and the atmosphere shifted into the high frequency of Almighty God's presence. When the music modulated, our voices reached a crescendo, and became one in the harmonies of Heaven. We were all absorbed into His love.

I was praying in the spirit, and suddenly I was seeing into Heaven! Not with my natural eyes, but with my Spiritual eyes. I saw Kitty already there with Jesus, my mom, my dad, and my sister, Keithe! They were all smiling and rejoicing. They were also praying for us. I saw big strong angels who sang "Holy, Holy, Holy." As I was seeing these things I was telling the family what I saw. Then I began laughing with such overwhelming joy. Everyone was being filled with the joy of the Lord and began laughing also. I knew Kitty's body was right here in front of us, but the revelation that her Spirit was already with her Lord and Savior, Jesus, was overwhelmingly joyful! I began to prophesy to several of my family for healing, and restoration. I saw hearts being healed from trauma. God was doing an amazing thing right in the midst of us.

At about 2:00 a.m., the anointing lifted, and we all hugged each other and went out of the room to fellowship about what we'd just experienced. Each one had felt a real change in their hearts. My prayer was that the change and touch of the Lord would continue in my family's hearts and lives.

Saturday was a very good day for all of us. We were different. We no longer felt the pain of Kitty suffering, but the joy and peace that her spirit was already with the Savior. We continued giving her the medicine, talking to her and sitting with her. The Hospice nurses came and said it could be any time for Kitty to pass. We all stayed close to her all day and night.

I was exhausted emotionally and physically. Michael and Mona came by again to see Kitty that evening. Michael had been sick, so they stayed for 30 minutes. Stephen, Michelle, Tiffany, and most of my children were at the house watching and waiting, praying, and fellowshipping with each other. I finally said that I had to go to bed. It was about midnight. I had finally fallen asleep and was at peace.

At 1:00 a.m. on Sunday, September 11, 2022, Heather came into my room and told me I needed to come downstairs because Kitty's breathing was shallow, and was slowing down. I got up and went to Kitty's room. Stephen and the family were all in her room. Stephen turned to me and said, "I feel like it is important for you to be with Mom when she takes her last breath, so we're all going to step out of the room and let this be your time. You two came in the world together and it's appropriate for you to be there when she takes her last breath and leaves this world." This was such a selfless act by Stephen and Michelle as Kitty's children. This deeply touched my heart.

I went to Kitty's bed and asked Jennifer if she would help me get up into the bed with Kitty. She helped me up, and I put my arms around her. I began to tell Kitty how very much I loved her and how much I would miss her. I kissed her several times and held her close. I was watching her shallow breathing; in, out, in, out, in, out, then no in. I just laid there holding her. I kissed her again and said "it's over."

She passed on at approximately 1:20 a.m. I stepped down out of the bed, walked outside the room, and said to Stephen "it's over, she's gone." We hugged, and I hugged Michelle, and my kids, and thanked them for all they had done for Kitty, and for supporting me. Jennifer helped me up the stairs, and I went back to bed.

Stephen called Hospice, and they came over, and a hearse also came to take Kitty's body. It was Kitty's desire to donate her skin to burn victims which we did. Heather came upstairs and asked me if I wanted to come down and say goodbye to Kitty. I said no. I had said my goodbyes, and I really didn't think I could take seeing her in a bag and leaving. Kitty was already in the presence of Jesus, and her fleshly body was of no use now. She had requested to be cremated. We were going to see that it was done.

Sunday morning, we all got up and felt a heavy weight had just been lifted. In many ways we felt sad that we wouldn't see her anymore, but we felt such relief in knowing that she was eternally with Jesus. These days and nights with our family supporting Stephen and Michelle, helping with Kitty's care, and praying and worshipping the Lord were priceless. We all had experienced a God encounter that changed us. I warned the family of a backlash that may come from Satan, and strongly advised them to get in God's Word, and continue to pray.
Several other family members came to Stephen's at this time. We all shared lunch, and many joyful memories of Kitty. We took a picture together with a shirt that said, "No One Fights Alone". We de-

cided this would be our family motto. We all prayed together, hugged and said, "I love you a bushel and a peck." It was difficult leaving this place of safety with our family and God, but we had to get back to our own homes, and work.

Stephen worked tirelessly to get pictures of Kitty's life together for the Celebration of Life service. He had a short video of Kitty telling what songs she wanted sung at the service and what songs she wanted for the video of the pictures.

The day before Kitty's Celebration our nieces, Chrissy and Terri, who were our oldest sister's girls, flew in for the service. Because Kitty was always asking new nurses or aids if they knew Jesus, we decided to have a banner made that said, "Do You Know Jesus? Love, Kitty." When our nieces arrived, we were out in the yard holding this banner. They said, "Yes we do!" We all laughed and hugged. We hung the banner over the mantel for all to see.

On the day of Kitty's celebration service, we had decided to have her grave side service with just family, and Kitty's two best friends Judy Burns, and Susan Newman in Muskogee where she had lived most of her life. We live there so it was good for me, and our sister Candy knowing we could frequently visit the site. We decided this would be a good time for any of us that had songs they wanted to play, or words of remembrance they wanted to say to do so. It was a very emotional time for each of us. The songs that were played were all about God, and love. There were few words spoken due to emotions. But right in the middle of our service a deer appeared in the distance which was looking right at us.

The funeral director said he had conducted hundreds of grave sides, but he had never ever seen a deer show up. Immediately we started to sing the song, "As a Deer Panteth for the Water." The lyrics of that song express what Kitty's heart felt, and what our hearts were feeling.

"As the deer panteth for the water So my soul longeth after Thee You alone are my heart's desire And I long to worship Thee.
[Refrain]

"You alone are my strength, my shield To You alone may my spirit yield You alone are my heart's desire And I long to worship Thee."
Martin Nystrom, 1984 Based on Psalm 42

That afternoon we held Kitty's Celebration Service at Victory Christian Chapel in Tulsa. All of Kitty's family, and my family were there, plus our two nieces, Chrissy, and Terri, and Kitty's best friend, Judy. When Pastor Sharon Daugherty came in the family room she was taken back when she saw me because Kitty and I looked so much alike. Pastors Sharon and Paul Daugherty conducted the service. Pastor Sharon led us in singing How Great Thou Art, and Great Are You Lord. Pastor Paul sang a song he had written that Kitty especially liked and had requested.

Then I came to the platform to share a few of my memories. I shared several of my twin stories, but my favorite was about embarrassing our dad. We were five or six years old and loved to ride bare back on our neighbor's horse. One day Kitty and I were riding double and bare back up to the Muskogee Country Club where dad was playing golf with executives from Brockway Glass Company. We didn't know if we would see him or not, but we did. There we were on a hot Oklahoma summer day with no tops on, wearing only shorts, boots, and our cowgirl hats sitting atop a horse. When we saw our dad we shouted out, "Hi Daddy!" He was startled to see us. He couldn't deny that these rag-a-muffins were his little girls.

Stephen and Michelle shared some memories about their mom, too. Michael chose not to share. He had been very emotional at the grave side. Pastor Sharon shared encouraging, and comforting words from the Word of God, and a salvation invitation.

Then they began to show the video of Kitty's life. Kitty had requested "Some Where Over the Rainbow" by Israel Kamakawiwo'Ole, "What a Wonderful World," by Louis Armstrong, and "Don't Worry Be Happy" by Bobby McFerrin to be played with her video. I completely fell apart hearing these songs, and seeing our birth, and baby pictures. I wept and wept as I saw the life we had mostly shared together. Wayne, and our son, Jonathan, held me and comforted me. Again, I was facing the reality of Kitty's death.

Afterward, we greeted friends of Kitty's in the foyer, and then we all went to Stephen's house for dinner. Kitty's friends were so very nice and sympathetic to me. Kitty's friends Susan and Tom Neuman were there also. Judy and I sat down to eat, and talked more about how very much we would miss Kitty. The children played in the back yard as if nothing had happened. They were all cousins and were totally enjoying each other, which is just what Kitty would have wanted.

After the guests left, our family all hugged and prayed together about the task of getting Kitty's house ready for sale and distributing her things. We said goodbye to our dear nieces, Chrissy, and Terri, as they prepared to fly back home. I wondered what the coming days would be like for me without Kitty. I knew I needed to stay close to Stephen, Michael, and Michelle. Stephen was charged with organizing and completing everything connected to Kitty. He would definitely be in my prayers. He had been especially close to his mom, and he would grieve the hardest.

Kitty was victorious in her life and in her death. God kept His Word to her. She was given the highest level of healing by the Lord for being "absent in the body is to be present with the Lord" (2 Corinthians 5:8, KJV). No matter what harsh situations she had to deal with she always worshipped God amidst her pain, and tears. She continues to dance with her Father God in fields of grace, worshipping, and adoring Him. Here's to my sweet Kitty; I only miss you when I breathe.

14
Where Did He Come From?

In the early summer of 2020 Wayne and I lost our Maltese dog, Molly, and Chihuahua, Macey. Both passed away from old age. It was very upsetting and emotional for Wayne and me. Wayne said we couldn't get another dog because it was too upsetting losing them since they were such an integral part of our family. I was insistent that I had to have another dog. I had never been without a dog, except in college, and I couldn't be without one now. Our animals had always been such a joy to us.

We had five children, and at one point we had five dogs, too. Once we had a Beagle named Sadie, a Chihuahua named Charlie, a Golden Retriever named Regis, a Blue Heeler named Lady, and a Dachshund named Daisy. We also had a cat named Jeremy, one named Angel, and one named Delilah.

Most were outside pets. We loved animals. We also had two horses. We had a Tennessee Walking horse, which I showed at fairs, and a Quarter horse that Wayne used to cut with at the Round Up Club events and for trail rides.

Since we had grown older, we hadn't had time for the horses, so we had to sell them. We really missed riding. The cats died at different times, and so did the dogs. We had Molly and Macey after most of the kids were all grown and gone. So, when they passed away, I prayed every day that God would either soften Wayne's heart for us to have a dog or give me His grace to live without one. BUT GOD had His own plan.

In August of 2020, I was out running errands, and came home, and parked my car under the tree beside the street. I looked up at the front porch and saw a dog sitting there. I got out of the car and went to the porch to see the dog. It was a male, freshly groomed, without a collar. His hair was strawberry blonde just like my hair!

He was so pretty and friendly! I opened the front door, and he shot right into our house. His tail was wagging, and he was jumping up on me wanting attention. He was so very sweet. I sat down and he jumped in my lap. He seemed to be laughing! Wayne was in the den, so I picked up this energetic dog and took him into the den to meet Wayne. He gave me that look like what have you done? I explained how the dog was on our front porch, and he didn't have a collar.

He immediately said, "Well he had to come from somewhere; He's freshly groomed." The dog pawed at Wayne's chest and licked his face. He was such a happy dog! Yet Wayne said I had to look for the owner.

That night we put the dog in a dog carrier. He was not happy about that. He fussed most of the night. The next day I took him to a vet to see if he had a chip, but he didn't. The veterinarian said he was a Cairn Terrier about 2-3 years old. My daughter, Heather, and I then put up a few posters in our neighborhood with our contact information, but no one contacted us.

After three days I asked Wayne if we could please keep this dog? He had enjoyed this friendly little guy as much as I had. He finally said yes! I was ecstatic! God had answered my prayers! "Delight yourself in the Lord, and He will give you the desires of your heart" (Psalm 37:4, NASB).

Now we could give him a name. We thought of several names, but the name that described his sweet face was 'Chewbacca'. It was easier to just call him Chewy. Wayne said this was my dog, and I was responsible for taking care of him. He wasn't completely house-trained, so I was constantly on the watch. But the interesting thing was that Chewy kept following Wayne around.

In the morning Wayne would put him outside, then when he came back in, he followed Wayne to the bathroom and sat outside the door while Wayne was showering and getting ready for the day. Chewy followed him into the bedroom while he got dressed. Then when Wayne left for work Chewy would come and jump up on the foot of our bed and lay down until I got up.

When I was at home Chewy would sit on my lap in my recliner, and periodically lick my face. We had a bed for him that he used during the day. Around 5:00 p.m. he would go to the kitchen door and sit. Then he'd start whining and pacing in the kitchen. Suddenly Wayne would open the door, and Chewy would get so excited!

He jumped on him and kept showing his excitement by vigorously wagging his tail and turning in circles! Wayne would go into the living room and sit down on the couch, and Chewy would jump up on Wayne's lap wanting to tussle with Wayne. Wayne would play with him for a good fifteen minutes each night with Chewy growling, and softly biting in fun.

To this day, almost four years later, Chewy still follows this routine. He and Wayne are the best of buddies. He sleeps on a towel at the end of our bed each night. He's a good little guard dog, but his only fault is that he gets so excited to see family that he jumps on them and tinkles a little on the floor. So, when family comes over, we put a belly band on him, then no one gets offended.

It continues to amaze me how God cares so much about the little things in our lives, our unspoken thoughts, and how He's so happy to grant them to us. I am so very grateful to my Heavenly Father. He has kept me, my husband, my children, my grandchildren, my relatives, and all my friends. I have seen the glory of God manifest in so many ways, that I cannot tell it all. If I had a thousand tongues, I could not praise Him enough. There are not enough words in all the books in the world to describe or express how good and great God is.

Therefore, as I end this book let it be known that God's love, goodness, grace, and power never fails. If the devil had his way, I should have been discouraged, I should have failed, I should have given up and I should have lost all hope and my faith. But when I look back over my life, what the devil meant for evil, God turned it around for my good. With that, all I can truly say is, I never would have made it…BUT GOD!

"O Lord, You have examined my heart and know everything about me. You know when I sit down or stand up. You know my thoughts even when I'm far away. You know what I am going to say even before I say it, Lord."
Psalm 139:1-2,4, NLT

"But thou, O Lord, art a shield for me; my glory, and the lifter of mine head."
Psalms 3:3 KJV

...BUT GOD

My Testimony

Thank you God, I'm healed from sickness and disease.

I am delivered and I am set free.

It's not for one, no not just for me,

But for my children, and for their seed.

It's by Christ's blood that He shed,

That I'm healed from my toes, to my head.

Delivered from worries, and from all fears,

Showing my thankfulness through my tears.

God has given me joy and filled me with His glory,

This is my testimony and deliverance story!

by
Suzie Buck

Suzie's Favorite Scriptures

Isaiah 54:17
No weapon formed against you shall prosper, and every tongue which rises against you in judgement you shall condemn. This is the heritage of the servants of the Lord, and their righteousness is from Me, says the Lord.

Isaiah 53:5
But He was wounded for our transgressions, He was bruised for our iniquities: the chastisement of our peace was upon Him; and with His stripes we are healed.

Matthew 19:26
Jesus said, "With man this is impossible, but with God all things are possible."

James 5:16
Pray one for another so that you may be healed.

Ephesians 2:4-5
But God is so rich in mercy, and He loved us so much, that even though we were dead because of our sins, He gave us life when He raised Christ from the dead. (It is only by God's grace that you have been saved!)

Ephesians 6:10-11

Finally, my brethren, be strong in the Lord and in the power of His might. I put on the whole armor of God, that I may be able to stand against the wiles of the devil.

Psalm 91

He who dwells in the secret place of the Most High shall abide under the shadow of the Almighty. I will say of the Lord, "He is my refuge and my fortress; my God, in Him I will trust." Surely He shall deliver me from the snare of the fowler and from the noisome pestilence. He shall cover me with His feathers, and under His wings I shall take refuge; His truth shall be my shield and buckler. I shall not be afraid of the terror by night, nor of the arrow that flies by day nor of the pestilence that walks in darkness, nor of the destruction that lays waste at noonday. A thousand may fall at my side, and ten thousand at my right hand; but it shall not come near me. Only with my eyes shall I look, and see the reward of the wicked. Because I have made the Lord, who is my refuge, even the Most High, my dwelling place, no evil shall befall me, nor shall any plague come near my dwelling. For He shall give His angels charge over me, to keep me in all my ways. In their hands they shall bear me up, lest I dash my foot against a stone. I shall tread upon the lion and the cobra,

the young lion and the cobra, the young lion and the serpent I shall trample underfoot. "Because you have set your love upon Me, therefore I will deliver you; I will set you on high, because you have known My name. You shall call upon Me, and I will answer you; I will be with you in trouble; I will deliver you and honor you.
With long life I will satisfy you and show you My salvation."

Acts 10:34
…God is no respecter of persons.

Psalm 103:1-5
Bless the Lord, O my soul: and all that is within me bless His holy name. Bless the Lord, O my soul, and forget not all his benefits: who forgiveth all thine iniquities; who healeth all thy diseases; who redeemeth thy life from destruction; who crowneth thee with lovingkindness and tender mercies; who satisfieth thy mouth with good things; so that thy youth is renewed like the eagle's.

Psalm 107:20
I sent My word and healed you and delivered you from destructions.

Jeremiah 30:17
I will restore health unto you, and I will heal you of your wounds saith the Lord.

Matthew 15:26
Healing is the children's bread.

Luke 10:19
Behold, I give you authority over all the enemy's power and nothing shall by any means hurt you.

1 Peter 2:24
By My stripes you were healed.

2 Peter 1:3
My divine power has given unto you all that pertain unto life and godliness through the knowledge of Me.

Proverbs 3:5-6
Trust in the Lord with all thine heart; and lean not unto thine own understanding. In all thy ways acknowledge Him, and He shall direct they paths.

Deuteronomy 31:6
So be strong and courageous! Do not be afraid and do not panic before them. For the Lord your God will personally go ahead of you. He will neither fail you nor abandon you.

Isaiah 41:10
So do not fear, for I am with you; do not be dismayed, for I am your God. I will strengthen you and help you; I will uphold you with my righteous right hand.

Philippians 4:6
Be anxious for nothing, but in everything by prayer and supplication with thanksgiving, let your requests be made known unto God.

Isaiah 55:11
So shall My word be that goeth forth out of My mouth: It shall not return unto me void, but it shall accomplish that which I please, and It shall prosper in the thing whereto I sent it.

Philippians 4:13
I can do all things through Christ who strengthens me.

Philippians 4:19
But my God shall supply all your needs according to His riches in glory by Christ Jesus.

About the Author

Suzanne C. Buck, known by friends as Suzie, is a devout woman of God who sees God in everything in her life. She has been married to her husband, Wayne, for 54 years, and has 5 amazing children, Heather Buck, Jennifer Jones, Whitney Coleman, Andrea Milligan, and Jonathan Buck. She has 12 grandchildren, and 7 great grandchildren who are her passion. She and her husband serve on the worship team of Kingdom Church in Broken Arrow, Oklahoma. She is a nationally certified Speech-Language Pathologist who taught in Muskogee Public Schools for 21 years, and also worked part-time in Home Health. Currently she works part-time at St. Joseph Catholic School in Muskogee, Oklahoma as a Speech-Language Pathologist. Suzanne also volunteers as a Court Appointed Special Advocate (CASA) for children in Foster Care. For fun she line dances with the Sassy Steppers.

ABOUT THE PUBLISHER

Let Life to Legacy bring your story to literary life! We offer the following publishing services: manuscript development, editing, transcription services, ghost-writing, cover design, copyright services, ISBN assignment, worldwide distribution, and eBook conversion. Throughout production, we keep the author informed every step of the way. Even if you do not have a manuscript, that's not a problem for us. We can ghost-write your book from audio recordings or legible handwritten documents. Whether print on demand or trade publishing, we have packages to meet your publishing needs. At Life to Legacy, we take the stress out of becoming a published author. Unlike other so-called publishers, we do more than just print books. Our books and eBooks are distributed to book buyers, distributors, and online retailers throughout the world. This is real publishing! Call us today for a free quote.

Please visit our website
www.Life2Legacy.com
or call us
708-272-4444
Send email inquiries
Life2Legacybooks@att.net

www.ingramcontent.com/pod-product-compliance
Lightning Source LLC
Chambersburg PA
CBHW031601110426
42742CB00036B/608